PRAISE FOR *THE RESCUER*

"This book will change your life. Why? Because it is just so real, raw, vulnerable, provocative, honest, and visceral. Jason's life and story cannot help but draw you in and transform you. What makes this book so powerful is that in the midst of all the struggles and danger, you cannot miss the beautiful story of redemption and hope. I am very happy to have read this book. You will be too!"

—DANIEL FUSCO, PASTOR, TELEVISION AND RADIO HOST,
AUTHOR OF *CRAZY HAPPY* AND *UPWARD, INWARD, OUTWARD*

"Incredibly raw . . . we repeatedly laughed and cried. . . . This book captures the harrowing and heart-wrenching life of a firefighter/first responder, and how he discovered that ultimately he was the one who needed to be rescued."

—JOHNNY AGAR, AUTHOR, MOTIVATIONAL SPEAKER,
UNDER ARMOUR AMBASSADOR

"Jason Sautel is the real deal. He is a real man with real stories about real transformation. Everything you read in this book comes from the soul of a person who lives life fully every step of the way."

—LANCE C. HAHN, SENIOR PASTOR,
BRIDGEWAY CHRISTIAN CHURCH, ROSEVILLE CA

"*The Rescuer* is a beautiful story about the pain and suffering that sometimes steer us to the most wonderful parts of our lives. Jason writes about his pain and struggles, and how they ultimately led him not only to his amazing wife but to his Lord and Savior. I couldn't put this book down."

—JENNIFER HOPPING, WIFE, MOM, KINDERGARTEN TEACHER

"As a fellow first responder, I have seen and felt the darkness that Jason mentions. *The Rescuer* is inspiring, and it shows how the love of a good woman and the Lord can change a man and save him."

—DEPUTY SCOTT BROWN, SACRAMENTO COUNTY SHERIFF'S OFFICE

"I can't recommend this book enough to anyone who feels lost, has been saved or been the one to save, loves firefighter stories, questions their faith, or just wants to read about how one man made it out of the darkness through faith."

—SARA M., TRAINING SPECIALIST

"Jason's testimony is honest, raw, and inspiring. His story will benefit first responders of all backgrounds by reminding them that life is possible after so much loss."

—BRANDON MATTSON, FIREFIGHTER/PARAMEDIC

"Jason Sautel is one of the most interesting people I've ever met. At a time when good storytelling is hard to find, this guy's testimony is a breath of fresh air. *The Rescuer* is quite a redemption tale, and it's just the tip of the Sautel iceberg. Can't wait to see what he does next."

—ROB ELLIOTT, PASTOR

"Jason explains well the closeness firefighters develop at the dinner table. It also struck me how much courage it took to write something so personal and revealing about his home life. He is sharing a very emotional part of his life with the world and those of us who know him. This book examines the close living situations of our fire department and the complex events we encounter in a very credible way. He carefully weaves a tale that encompasses the heart of his experiences in the service.

Though Jason is careful to make his characters generic, I can see some of my influence in his life. We take mentorship seriously at the firehouse, and I hope what we try to teach will help our family. I watched Jason grow and saw the change that came over him when Kristie came into his life. He became a whole new person. I would like to think there were a few things I have said that also encouraged him down that path. I am so glad he has prospered and is willing to share his experiences. This is how we pay it forward and mentor. Jason is now the mentor, and though he has left the department, he is still completing one of the most important tasks we are given as firefighters."

—LIEUTENANT SHERRI BANKS (RETIRED)

THE
RESCUER

THE
RESCUER

ONE FIREFIGHTER'S STORY OF COURAGE, DARKNESS, AND THE RELENTLESS LOVE THAT SAVED HIM

JASON SAUTEL

WITH D. R. JACOBSEN

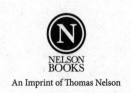

NELSON
BOOKS

An Imprint of Thomas Nelson

Published in Nashville, Tennessee, by Nelson Books, an imprint of Thomas Nelson. Nelson Books and Thomas Nelson are registered trademarks of HarperCollins Christian Publishing, Inc.

Published in association with literary agent Tawny Johnson of Illuminate Literary Agency, http://illuminateliterary.com.

Thomas Nelson titles may be purchased in bulk for educational, business, fund-raising, or sales promotional use. For information, please e-mail SpecialMarkets@ThomasNelson.com.

Scripture quotations are taken from the Holy Bible, New Living Translation. © 1996, 2004, 2015 by Tyndale House Foundation. Used by permission of Tyndale House Publishers, Inc., Carol Stream, Illinois 60188. All rights reserved.

Any Internet addresses, phone numbers, or company or product information printed in this book are offered as a resource and are not intended in any way to be or to imply an endorsement by Thomas Nelson, nor does Thomas Nelson vouch for the existence, content, or services of these sites, phone numbers, companies, or products beyond the life of this book.

Library of Congress Cataloging-in-Publication Data

Names: Sautel, Jason, 1974- author.
Title: The rescuer: one firefighter's story of courage, darkness, and the relentless love that saved him / Jason Sautel; with D. R. Jacobsen.
Description: Nashville, Tennessee : Thomas Nelson, [2020] | Summary: "The true story—told with heart-pounding action and heart-melting romance—of a heroic firefighter forced to confront an emergency even he can't handle: saving himself"—Provided by publisher.
Identifiers: LCCN 2019050443 (print) | LCCN 2019050444 (ebook) | ISBN 9781400216475 (HC) | ISBN 9781400216482 (ePub)
Subjects: LCSH: Fire fighters. | Fire extinction. | Rescues.
Classification: LCC HD8039.F5 S378 2020 (print) | LCC HD8039.F5 (ebook) | DDC 363.37092--dc23
LC record available at https://lccn.loc.gov/2019050443
LC ebook record available at https://lccn.loc.gov/2019050444

Printed in United States of America

20 21 22 23 24   LSC   10 9 8 7 6 5 4 3 2 1

This book is dedicated to anyone who is lost, hurt, and lonely. I want you to know that the hope I found is there for you too.

CONTENTS

CONTENTS

AUTHOR'S NOTE

I **WAS PRIVILEGED TO** serve the city of Oakland for nearly two decades as a first responder.

I started as an Alameda County paramedic, then soon joined the Oakland Fire Department (OFD) as a firefighter/paramedic. I worked in every district and firehouse across the city with hundreds of men and women who became my brothers and sisters, but I considered West Oakland my home district.

The events in this book took place while I was with the OFD during my twenties. Along the way I talk about danger and darkness. I talk about real fires that burned real victims. Real emergencies that took real lives. And I struggle with that because my story overlaps with other people's pain—with people who maybe don't want strangers reading about their kid or parent in harm's way. Or even dying.

I get that. These stories still hurt me, so I can only imagine how much worse it is for them. I don't want to add to that.

What makes the whole thing even more complicated is the internet. A bunch of my time with the OFD is online and searchable, with photos. That's why I've chosen to protect the identities of almost everyone in this book, from victims to bystanders to fellow first responders.

So if you served with me in Oakland and recognize a scene we were on together, chances are you'll find something "wrong" about the name or the street or the time of day. That's on purpose to protect the privacy and limit the potential pain of everyone involved. I keep our operational roles, policies, and procedures somewhat vague for the same reasons. And there's no Station 11 in Oakland. It's a hybrid station I created to capture the vibe of the most memorable stations I served in. So if I tell the story of a nighttime incident on Ninety-Eighth Avenue and you know it *actually* happened during the day on San Pablo Boulevard, you're right! But now you know that the change is intentional, and it's for what I hope are good reasons.

JASON

CHAPTER 1

A BRIDGE TO EVIL

WHEN A STRUCTURE IS on fire, you can see the danger *and* plan a way to fight it.

As the fire spreads from a pile of dirty rags to a wall, then from the wall to the roof, you can gauge how much time you have before the whole building goes up in flames. Most times when you arrive on scene, you can make a quick plan of attack and execute it with your team. You can deploy equipment and resources where they'll do the most good. And, if the fire still grows, you can always call for additional alarms that will bring more fire engines and trucks.

But when a soul is on fire? How can a rescuer prevent a *life* from burning down?

As a veteran firefighter paramedic in Oakland, California, I was trained and equipped to deal with whatever emergency this screwed-up world decided to throw my way. I had been called to pull people from fires, to extinguish the flames . . . but I was slowly dying inside, and who would rescue me?

That was the question I never thought I'd be wrestling with so personally. I had never let anyone into my world long enough to offer me the help I needed. My days and nights were a never-ending cycle of bringing relief to others and stockpiling pain for myself.

I started fighting fires at eighteen as a volunteer in a small desert community in Southern California. Tenth grade was when school and me decided to go our separate ways, and when my high school class graduated, I watched the ceremony from across the street, sitting on top of my fire engine. I went from volunteering straight into paramedic school at nineteen. That took me to a paramedic ambulance company in San Bernardino, California, and within a few months I scored a job in Oakland as an Alameda County paramedic. A couple years later I passed the Oakland Fire Department's entrance exam.

The entrance exam was rigorous—a written test, a verbal test, oral interview boards, psychological tests, strict medical exams, and background checks. Few made it through. Those of us who did weren't *better* than anyone else, but maybe we knew how to suffer more. Then it was sixteen weeks at the training academy throwing ladders, pulling hoses, and running up the seven stories to the top of the training tower carrying every imaginable piece of heavy firefighting equipment, pausing only long enough to vomit. Graduation welcomed us into twelve months of probation before we became permanent members of Oakland Fire.

Our crew at Station 11 in West Oakland took pride in never making the job about us. Our job was to serve others. Period. With four hundred thousand residents packed together, there were plenty of opportunities for mayhem. Like scores of murders every year, not to mention countless shootings and stabbings where the victims lived to see another day. Men beat up women and each other. Kids were hurt. There were accidents of every imaginable kind: hit-and-runs, head-on collisions, trees blown over by gusty winds, electrocutions, heart attacks, chemical exposure . . . the list went on and on. The next rescue, the next call, the next chance to make a difference. That's what we did as a team. Our job was to keep pushing.

There were four of us on my shift at Station 11, and two other shifts made sure the station was staffed 24/7. Cappy was our captain, Roger—we called him Rog—was our engineer/driver, and Jimmy was our firefighter, along with me. All of us were EMTs, plus I was a licensed paramedic. That meant I could administer medications and do advanced life support, and the EMTs would assist me. In a hospital, a surgeon is useless without a highly trained and supportive medical team, and it was the same with us in the field. One difference, though, was that the four of us needed to wear multiple hats and stay flexible, because we never knew what the streets might throw our way.

Each of us was there because we chose to be. Me and the guys were as hard as the place we served. We had to be if we didn't want to get eaten alive. At the firehouse it was all fun and games, but when we rolled out the door on an emergency response, we transformed into stone-cold lifesavers.

If I was honest with myself, though, saving lives wasn't my only motivation. The excitement of my job helped numb the pain of my past. Firefighting was my drug. The adrenaline of responding to a call helped me forget the darkness that was always lurking nearby.

For me, life had always been more shadow than sunlight. No real friends. Constantly arguing with my dad. Gut-punching loss when my mom moved five hundred miles away after they divorced. My sister moved too—first away with my mom, then later, clear across the country to North Carolina. I slept on a mattress with more stains on it than blankets. I was only ten years old the first time I considered suicide. I'd never been in a romantic relationship that didn't end in pain.

Working as a firefighter, I still kept all that locked up inside me. Almost nothing could crack my public armor. And if something did, like a rougher-than-usual emergency, I'd bury my pain even deeper. Bro it up. Shrug. Crack wise. Go out drinking with the guys or chase girls . . . anything to try and fill the emptiness inside me. But it never lasted, never really worked, so I'd just hit my job even harder.

My life was about as good as I could expect. I had an important job I was good at. I had a group of buddies. Whenever my personal pain flared up, I always managed to stamp it down.

Until one day I responded to a scene that made me realize my life was already an emergency, and there was no help in sight.

—◇—

The sound of the firehouse bell interrupted the four of us. We'd been lounging around the kitchen table like usual, telling stories, drinking coffee, and making fun of each other. There's a special camaraderie inside a firehouse. If someone were to walk in off the street and hear us, they would think we hated each other, but it was just our way of releasing the stress of our long shifts. We might be making fun of a guy's cheap haircut or commenting on the way his *extra*-medium T-shirt highlighted his love handles. But the minute the alarm sounded, we were all business. I would die for any of the guys I had just been verbally abusing, and they would do the same for me.

The dispatch was for a suicidal jumper. Male. He was on the Bay Bridge during morning rush hour.

Sad to say, but this was not the first suicide attempt I'd responded to. In our city, with so many people suffering so much misery, it seemed like someone was constantly deciding there was no choice but to end it all. On the bright side, though, not a single one had ever killed themselves in front of me. I was always able to talk them down—either that or they were long dead before we arrived. I was confident this time would be no different.

Less than one minute after the call, we were on the engine and roaring into the street. Our engine was a snub-nosed beast. Rog always drove, Cappy navigated up front, and me and Jimmy sat in the rear, facing backward. New kids would stay safely seated and face back-ward, staring at the diamond plate, but once you had some fires under your belt, you wanted to size the situation when you were still a few blocks away. To see forward, we just stood up and spun around. I fig-ured if I fell off the engine, I probably couldn't handle fighting fires!

Since it was a medical call, there was no need for all the bulky gear we wore to fires. I was already dressed in my uniform: dark-blue and patched-up wool pants, polished steel-toed station boots, T-shirt with OAKLAND FIRE plastered on the back, and a light sweater to match. Out of tradition, I responded with my leather fireman's helmet on as well. You could tell how much fire a guy had seen by looking at his helmet. The more soot-covered, burned, and damaged, the better, because it meant you were a "worker" and not scared to take on a few burns and get dirty. Each guy's lid became a part of him, and over time the lids took on personalities.

Heading west out of Oakland, sitting high above the cars, I had a good vantage point. Regardless of what dispatch reported, you never knew exactly what kind of emergency scene awaited or how bad the situation really was. Back when I was a paramedic intern, I once asked my hard-core, old-school, Vietnam vet preceptor what we were responding to. "A *patient*!" he answered. "A patient that needs your help!" He trained me to keep my blinders off and not make too many assumptions.

Ahead I could see traffic backing up. Even with our lights and sirens, we were going nowhere fast. As we approached the rise of the Bay Bridge, driving at a snail's pace, I glanced down at a random com-muter creeping along beside us. The driver met my eyes and shrugged. We were just as stuck as he was, and there was nothing either of us could do about it. I thought about the jumper as I drummed my fin-gers on my leg. *Come on, come on.*

At last we arrived on scene. My boots had barely hit the con-crete when a CHP (California Highway Patrol) officer approached us. "Guys, we got a jumper, and the negotiator is on his way," he said, motioning me toward where the man was. As we walked, we both looked across the sea of parked cars on the bridge. The officer answered my unasked question, "No firm ETA on the negotiator." Both of us knew what that meant. It would be up to my team to save the jumper.

As the CHP officer gave me a rundown on the situation, I glimpsed the man for the first time. I could see him through a semi-circle of emergency personnel. He was on the other side of the railing, standing on a ledge no wider than his sneakers. He kept one hand tightly clutched to the guardrail. His knuckles were white but his fingers were red. He was terrified. It was obvious he had been holding that rail for quite a while.

Suicidal people are patients, not criminals. For whatever reason, the world has failed to give them the care and compassion they need. Either that or these folks have been told so many lies that they can't hear or feel the help being offered to them. Point is, they always need help. Someone has to show up and give them hope. Sounds easy, except it isn't. I reached the railing about ten feet from the man and looked over the edge. *Sautel, it's not the height you should be scared of . . . it's the fall!*

The jumper appeared completely normal. He was in jeans, a T-shirt, and tennis shoes and had short, dark hair and a scruffy beard. He could have been anyone in Oakland. He could have been me.

I let go of the railing and stepped into the moment. Holding up my hands, palms out, I said, "Hey, bro. I'm just a fireman, not a cop, okay?" It was my classic opening line. "All *I* have to keep me safe is a cool personality," I continued, motioning my head at the CHP officers behind me, "not a gun."

The man looked at me and laughed. He shook his head like he couldn't believe what he was hearing. Which was exactly what I wanted. It meant he was focused on me rather than his circumstances or surroundings. That was good, because his surroundings were both gorgeous and totally terrifying. It was a clear day, with blue Pacific water stretching below. Unfortunately, our view was from hundreds of feet above the water with no safety net. Anything I could do to move him back toward the middle of the bridge would be a win.

"Can I come closer," I asked, "so we don't have to shout at each other?"

"Sure, man," he answered. He still seemed weirded out to be talking to someone like me. He didn't meet my eyes, but anything relational was good. Baby steps.

I eased along the railing until I was five feet away. I'd been trained to approach jumpers extremely slowly and only after asking. There's no sense in trying to get close only to spook someone and have them panic. I could tell from the lingo and the sounds over my shoulder that my crew was rigging up a harness for me. If we decided I should go over the railing, they'd need to tie me in first. No sense in losing two lives while trying to save one. We also had a truck company on the way from another station in case we needed more manpower to bring the jumper back.

I didn't think we would need the harness or the extra men. It was shaping up to be a pretty simple incident. Based on my experience, we were already close to a solution. It might take five more minutes, or even fifteen, but establishing trust was the biggest hurdle. Without trust there was no telling what a jumper might do. With trust, though, his story could have a happy ending. He could look up, meet my eyes, and nod, and I'd know it was time to offer my hand and help him climb back over the railing.

I could be a chatty guy. In cases like this, I could talk practically forever, my voice friendly and even the whole time. Where the person was from, what their job was, if they thought McGwire and Canseco had been juicing, and if so, did they care. I could stretch stuff like that to thirty minutes or more. I just needed to get the guy talking long enough to be comfortable. I took a quick look over my shoulder at my crew and gave a subtle nod. *We got this.*

I turned back toward the man. He was looking across the bay, so I did too. "What a day," I said calmly. He nodded like he was agreeing. Then he turned back toward me and looked at my chest instead of my eyes, just like he'd been doing all along. It seemed like he might be getting ready to accept help, so I continued the small talk. "Day like this makes you wonder if—"

The jumper's head snapped up, and his eyes locked on to mine. They were silently screaming. Not just with fear. Anyone would be scared in that situation, unless they were drunk or high, and this guy was completely sober. There was something else in his eyes besides fear. Maybe some*one* else. It was as if there was another being inside that poor man, looking out through his eyes and straight into me. I flinched. I wanted to look away but couldn't. I'd caught glimpses before of whatever was tormenting this man, but I'd never seen it in such detail.

People called 911 when they hoped to be saved, sure, but it was also the hopeless hotline. I'd been face-to-face with plenty of hopeless people, and their hopelessness showed in the way they moved and talked. It stared out of their eyes.

This guy didn't look away. Something in him was begging me for help, but something else was feasting on his fear.

"I'm sorry."

He said those two words like he meant them from the bottom of his heart. And also like he couldn't prevent what was about to happen.

Before I could move, or even speak, the man let go of the railing and took a step. Our eyes locked, and I could still see the pure evil behind his. Death with a capital *D*.

He hadn't wanted this, but he couldn't stop it. The splash was tiny. The sound was lost in the growl of traffic and the wind. A fall from that height kills nearly every jumper instantly. In the rare case the fall isn't fatal, the cold water and severe injuries finish the job.

I turned away. My guys and the other first responders had backed up to give me space. Each of their faces was a mirror of the way I felt: total shock. No one said a word, including me. There was nothing to say.

What in the hell *was that?* I didn't believe in God or the Devil, but I knew for sure whatever drove that man to kill himself was all too real. Alive even. I'd looked into its eyes, and it had stared me down, while *both* of them fell into San Francisco Bay.

And I'd never seen it coming. I was so confident, so in control, yet I couldn't shake the feeling that whatever evil was in that jumper was the same thing inside me . . . the thing that had haunted me since I was ten years old. It had overpowered him, and for the first time, I sensed it could do the same to me. Watching the jumper had ripped the bandage off my life of fear, sadness, and pain. And now my wound was open to every ill that wanted to infect me.

The man had *wanted* to climb back to safety—I knew he had—but instead he jumped. Or was pushed by whatever had just stared me down.

Which was . . . what? Could *anyone* have saved the jumper? And what if I wasn't as strong as I thought? Could anyone save *me*?

The questions filled my mind. And so did the evil presence, like it was glad I'd finally figured out where things stood between us. I was on the same bridge, but I was a different man. Or maybe I was finally realizing that I was *no* different from the hopeless victims I failed to save.

I climbed wearily back onto the fire engine. The sun nearly blinded me as I squinted at the metal siding, but I could still make out the evil as it climbed in with me and sat down. It rode with me back to the firehouse. It waited while I showered. It rode shotgun in my truck for the forty-five-minute trip to my place in Santa Rosa.

That was the day I figured it out: my life was an emergency.

I knew that without something to help me—someone to help

me—I'd end up like that man on the bridge. Asking for help, and longing for rescue, but powerless against whatever was smoldering inside him.

Whatever it was, it was inside me, too, and had been all along.

CHAPTER 2

WHOSE FAULT WAS IT?

EVERY OAKLAND FIREHOUSE HAD its own flavor, each as diverse as the city we served. It could be a one- or two-story building, a single house with one engine or a double with both an engine and a ladder truck, and each was crewed by different numbers of firefighters.

What united every firehouse was its heart: the kitchen. That's where real life went down. Our eating area easily sat the four of us, plus extra chairs for guests. Our stove was the best of the best: a Wolf Challenger with six burners, a built-in griddle, and twin ovens. Complementing our Cadillac stove were three refrigerators, two for food and one entirely for condiments. Ladles, knives, and cutting boards all hung in a specific place on the wall, and woe to the rookie who put something away in the wrong place after doing dishes. Like every other firehouse, we hung our hats on the old OFD saying, "One hundred fifty years of tradition unimpeded by progress." Even if some smart guy came up with a better way to do something, we'd razz him until he shut up and then get back to doing it the way it had always been done.

We spent the majority of our time in that kitchen. Countless hours spun past as we told stories, did our best Dr. Phil impressions for guys having issues, and played round after round of cards or shook dice. It was always loud and almost always fun. We were family, and like any close-knit family, we had our share of disagreements, but if we couldn't hash it out in the kitchen, we could always go out back for an aggressive game of pickleball.

When we weren't responding to a call or enjoying some downtime, we'd usually be working in the apparatus bay, right outside the kitchen. The apparatus bay defined the middle of the firehouse, with watch room/office, captain's room, TV room, and kitchen on one side, and dorms and bathroom on the other. It housed our engine, and we stored and maintained all our fire gear there.

We took pride in our spotless, polished concrete floors, even though our battalion chief *hated* them ever since he'd stopped by to drop off our paychecks and slipped and fell on his ass. More times than not we'd leave the apparatus bay doors up during the morning because we'd all be out there checking tools, doing drills with the new kids, or hiding from any office jobs Cappy might stick us with. He hated pushing paper too, so he'd hustle to join the rest of us outside as soon as he finished his nerd work.

The apparatus bay also housed our gym, which was nothing more than a big square of red carpet we "found" on the side of the freeway, coincidentally right after cleaning up an accident scene that involved a flipped big rig that had been hauling rolls of carpet. We topped the carpet with a random stack of dumbbells, barbells, and weight plates, plus a few benches we'd repaired so many times their surfaces were more duct tape than leather.

There wasn't much else that mattered. A few wooden lockers outside our bathroom where we could store our civilian clothes. Standard-issue beds. A custom leather recliner for each of us in the TV room. A fenced parking lot outside the apparatus bay where we could park our personal vehicles during our shifts. And that was Station 11.

It was my home away from home. In fact, it was a lot better than my home—especially when the alarm bell hit, along with that welcome shot of adrenaline.

You know that uneasy feeling of being out of control when you're strapped in on a huge roller coaster? Like it's going to take you somewhere whether you like it or not, even if you're having second thoughts? I felt a bit like that whenever I headed out to a fire: nervous but also energized by the thrill. The difference was, I always knew it might be my last ride.

Fourteen hours had passed since I watched that man take his eternal dive. On the outside I was just another one of the guys. Throwing fake smiles and pretend laughs was simple for me. But on the inside I was a wreck.

Then the alarm hit. "Structure fire," dispatch announced over the station speaker. Then she said the important part: "twelve hundred block of fifty-fourth street."

"We're first due!" Cappy yelled, which meant we would be the first fire engine to arrive at the scene, even though two more from our surrounding stations would be hot on our heels. This was exactly what I needed. I never wanted anyone's house to burn, but experience taught me it was inevitable. And since it was going to happen, I wanted to be there to help—and help myself as well by racing into fire-attack mode.

It was 11:00 p.m., and Rog was driving the engine like a race car. The guy could scream by within two inches of a parked car without blinking. Me and Jimmy were in back gearing up. With one hand at a time grabbing on to a metal handle, I shrugged into my turnout coat. Then I fastened up the metal snaps and pulled the straps of my SCBA bottle over my shoulders. I left the mask and air hose hanging, because with only twenty minutes of air in the bottle, we had to make every breath count. I crammed my leather helmet on, then stood up and wrapped my ax belt around my waist, sliding my ax into place. I checked to make sure my gloves were in my coat pocket, then spun and stood. With my head above the cab I had a great vantage point. I could see the ember-filled smoke billowing above an orange glow. We were still six blocks away, but I could tell this fire was burning hot and fast.

Soon we turned left and rolled up, and I could see the fire already roaring out of the bungalow. Those bungalows were basically fires waiting to happen, and sometimes it felt like half the city lived in one. The heat of the flames had already shattered every window in the house, which meant its interior was fully involved. Never a good sign.

I'd geared up, but I was only mostly dressed for the situation. Back at the firehouse I'd been wearing wool uniform pants and station boots when the call came in. If I'd been wearing shorts and sports—our term for shorts, a T-shirt, and running shoes—I would've just jumped into my fireproof turnout pants, which were held up by those famous red suspenders firefighters always wear. We prioritized the speed of our responses, because fire burned on its own evil schedule and every second mattered. I'd seen drivers leave slower guys back at the station. When the bell hit off, it was go time, and we sometimes had to make the call to stick with the clothes we had on.

Rog braked hard, and Jimmy and I hit the ground. I was the nozzle-man, so Jimmy would help Rog hook up the engine to a hydrant and then meet me at the front door. Often, if the fire wasn't too intense, a couple of responders from another engine or truck company would strap on their SCBAs and enter the structure to perform a quick search while the arriving hose team stretched the lines and got ready. With this fire, though, there was zero chance anyone was entering without following a hose line, which meant we needed to get water on the fire pretty much yesterday. It got worse when we heard what the neighbors were screaming.

"Sharon's in there! Sharon's still in there!"

"Where's Sharon's baby girl?!"

It was down to the four of us. Our backup engines were less than a minute away, but that didn't change what we had to accomplish. I pulled 150 feet of hose out of the hose bed while Jimmy cut the front gate with a bolt cutter. I ran toward the front door, with Rog making sure there were no kinks in the hose that might kick out when we called for water.

Near the front door I set the nozzle down, pulled my helmet off, tugged my face mask on and tightened its straps, and crammed my helmet back on, along with my gloves. Then I pulled out my ax and pried the metal security door off its hinges. One barrier left.

I dropped my ax and kicked in the front door. Flames poured out over my head and lit the porch roof on fire. I crouched below the worst of the flames. Even though the flames were rolling over my head and upward into the night sky, the radiant heat was pushing out on me like an oven turned to broil. Two white plastic chairs on the porch to my left were doing a slow-motion fall as their legs melted like marshmallows in a campfire.

I picked up the hose line and yelled over my shoulder, "Water, water, water!"

I glimpsed Jimmy behind me on the line, primed to back me up as we pushed forward. Back at the engine, Rog pulled the lever that would send 125 gallons of water per minute racing toward me. I made sure the nozzle selector was set to straight stream, which gave us more penetration into the heat and flames without disturbing the heat layer. A nozzle set to fog pattern, on the other hand, could disrupt the thermal layer inside a structure fire and push all the heat from the ceiling down, causing severe burns or death to anyone inside.

I felt the hose harden in my grip as the water arrived. I aimed the nozzle at the melting chairs next to me, pulled the lever back, and the stream of water—*phwooshhh*—launched the melting chairs into the neighbor's yard.

Straight stream confirmed, I aimed the hose back into the entryway.

No time for nerves, Sautel.

"Go!" I yelled.

I laid water on the flames raging above me, and then we were inside, crawling into a nightmare. Near the front door—with so much active fire—I could barely make out a large space, probably a living room based on my past experience. I knocked the flames down so the two guys who were now behind me could search the room, but I was pretty sure they wouldn't find anyone. Eleven o'clock at night in a one-story Oakland bungalow meant a high probability of a single mom trying to sleep—*if* she was at home and not working a second shift somewhere—plus kids, also sleeping. That meant we needed to get down the hallway.

Visibility dropped to zero as we crawled down the hall. Staying low enough to avoid the heat boiling along the ceiling wasn't easy. I had to work in an area of nonlethal air less than three feet high, and since the carpet was melting, my damn uniform pants were attaching themselves to my knees. I blindly swept the floor to cool it as much as possible, then redirected my stream back at the ceiling and walls in a circular motion.

Push, push, push.

We reached a doorway. I shoved it open and instantly a wave of superheated air blasted Jimmy and me. *Tap, tap, tap.* Jimmy was letting me know he was right behind. Not because I would have stopped doing my job, but because he was a veteran. He knew it never hurt the morale of the guy on nozzle to have a buddy behind him. I'd done the same for him on countless fires.

Fire inside a house straight sucked. It was so much more than the heat from the flames. The enclosed structure would cause all the heat to build up inside and intensify. And, to make matters worse, whenever we opened a door, we'd feed oxygen to that hungry fire. So we'd try to stay low, where the temperature would usually be north of 500 degrees, and we'd *really* try not to disrupt the layer of superheated air trapped against the ceiling.

I hit the room with water from the doorway. *Tap, tap, tap.* Jimmy kept pushing me. Another doorway, another fiery room knocked down. Pretty soon we'd hit every room, but the air was still hundreds of degrees, and our visibility still sucked. I knew there was fire we couldn't see raging in the attic, but I also knew whatever crew had arrived after us would've put guys on the roof to cut ventilation holes, allowing the superheated gasses and smoke still trapped in the bungalow to escape.

Once the majority of the free-burning fire had been knocked down, I shut off my hose and dropped it. But even with my flashlight on, I couldn't see more than a foot in the dank blackness.

Tap, tap, tap. I tapped Jimmy back, and we split up to search. Maybe we weren't Einsteins, but we could calculate the math of life and death as well as anyone. The chance of locating a survivor was basically zero. Okay, it *was* zero. But we never worked like that was the case. From day one in the OFD, we'd been trained to give 100 percent to the community we were blessed to serve. In this case, that meant a full search for survivors. Period. And if the two of us split up, we could search twice as fast.

I crawled a few feet back to the first hallway door and entered the room. I felt something hard and hot beneath me: a burned bed. The springs jabbed my blistered knees as I traversed to the other side of the room. My gloves told me I'd found a closet door. A slight push and it collapsed into ashy fragments. I felt my way deeper into the closet.

"I got one!" I yelled to Jimmy. My gloved hand had encountered something small and soft. Soon I was back in the hallway, making my way to the living room. Emergency lights from the street strobed in through the missing front door and shattered windows. I could see a few guys standing, so I stood too. They must have vented the roof.

Just as I reached the front door, a senior captain from another fire engine stepped forward and put his hand on my chest. I stopped. I couldn't see jack through my mask, but I could make out his silhouette. He shook his head side to side. Kept his hand on my chest.

I didn't look down, but I understood why he'd stopped me. The small body cradled in my gloves had been burning just as long as the rest of the stuff in the house. But to me the body wasn't stuff. It had been someone I was meant to save. He was right, though. There was no reason to bring the lifeless child outside where it would traumatize the neighbors even more than they already were.

Bump. Someone had run into me from behind. The captain stopped Jimmy the same way he'd stopped me. Then the captain pointed to his right, across what had been the living room. I walked to the corner and set down my burden. Jimmy did the same. We'd found Sharon and her baby girl.

As paramedic of the crew, it was my job to pronounce victims deceased and fill out the necessary forms for the coroner. I would have to physically assess the victims and write down my findings on a patient-care report. The report had to be precise, and I had to treat them like any other medical patient.

Was the airway open?

Was the victim breathing?

Did the victim have a pulse?

Since "burned beyond all recognition" wasn't a medical term, the report took a long time.

Once the fire was out, we dumped our bottles and masks at the engine, then grabbed the defibrillator and EKG and headed back inside. With a pen and a clipboard, I described the severity of each burned body part as I did a full head-to-toe, back-to-front assessment of a dead mother and her probably five-year-old girl. Then I found a way to attach an EKG to confirm that they were in asystole. Flatline. I attached four electrodes to what had been a chest and side.

Do your job, I told myself. *This isn't the first time you've touched dead people.* It wasn't even the tenth or the hundredth. It was just that on this call I could picture exactly what had happened. The kid had tried to escape the flames by crawling into the closet. Jimmy had found the mom at the doorway of her bedroom. She'd been trying to get to her kid. She hadn't made it.

I could barely force my hand to complete the physical examination, let alone the paperwork that went along with it. It was like an overflowing mug of filth, and I was going to have to drink it all the way to the bottom.

At last I walked out through the front doorway. Water from what was left of the roof dripped down my neck. I stepped down onto the sidewalk and took a breath of cool night air. A crowd of neighbors still surrounded our engine and the other trucks that had responded. In the emergency lights they seemed to be flickering in and out of focus. I pinched the bridge of my nose and took another long breath.

Then I climbed onto our engine and closed my eyes.

The door of our apparatus bay crawled open. The firehouse was the firehouse, same as it ever was. The floor gleamed beneath the overhead fluorescent lights. Everything was just as we had left it when we headed out.

I climbed down from the engine. I pulled my SCBA bottle out of the brackets in my seat. It felt twice as heavy. I took a spare bottle from the rack next to the fire engine and replaced the empty one. Then I took my turnout coat outside and hosed it down. We only had one set of gear, and I wanted to wash the carcinogens off before I hung it back on our engine.

Then it was time for the hose procedures. The four of us worked together to drag the hose all the way out. We washed it down and hung it to dry on the hose rack. We then fitted lengths of clean, dry hose to the engine. Getting ready for the next fire was a never-ending dance.

When we finished, Cappy nodded at each of us in turn. Time to hit the showers.

As I opened the door to the kitchen, I smelled fresh coffee and inhaled—but then I heard the voice of Pastor Esposito. He was an OFD chaplain and ran a church down the block. He would stop by to check on us, usually after a rough fire or fatal car wreck. If I was lucky, he'd be busy with someone else and I could sneak past, grab a cuppa joe, and shower. My wool pants were coated in wet, incinerated muck. My T-shirt was drenched with sweat, and I was starting to shiver. I reeked of burned furniture, burned carpet, burned electronics, burned wood, burned paint, burned stuffed animals.

Of everything the fire had taken.

My head had a jackhammer inside it that was beating a nice, regular rhythm. Maybe it was all the carbon monoxide I'd choked down on the call, or maybe it was heat exhaustion. It was definitely a dose of heavy guilt.

I almost made it out before Pastor Esposito noticed me. "Hey, Jason?"

I swore mentally. *What a joke. Did he think I wanted to chitchat?* I pretended I hadn't heard him and kept walking toward the showers.

"Hey! Jason!"

I spun back to face him. "What!" I yelled. It wasn't a question. I spat the word at him like a curse.

"I just wanted to see if you were okay," he said kindly, "or if you wanted to talk."

What was he thinking? That if I shared my feelings with him it would somehow bring the victims back to life? What I *wanted* was to have gotten to that fire ten minutes sooner. What I *wanted* was not to have failed. What I *wanted* was to erase from my brain forever what it felt like to hold the lifeless body of a burned child in my arms.

None of that would happen. So what I wanted *instead* was a shower and a half-dozen Tylenol washed down with my coffee. And maybe a few minutes of sleep before the automatic lights came on as the bell rang to send us out wearing our cold, stinking, soaking-wet jackets to the next fire, the next shooting, the next rape.

I couldn't care less what the pastor was planning to say to me. It could have been the most insightful, helpful thing in the entire universe. It didn't matter. My response was predetermined. I walked toward Pastor Esposito and began providing him with some suggestions of my own, about how he could start living his life. Maybe if he wanted to actually help people, he should stop talking to me and start showing up to our fires with an extra helmet. Maybe if he wanted to make a difference in real life, he should stop telling people fairy tales about a supposedly loving God who seemed happy enough letting innocent people burn to death.

By then I was yelling, and Cappy had shown up.

"Maybe," I continued, all up in the pastor's face, "you should stop preaching and instead go f—"

"Jason!" interrupted Cappy. He stepped between us, took a long breath, then spoke in a calm voice, "Why don't you go grab that shower you need?"

It was phrased as a question but said as a direct order. I turned and walked away. At knifepoint I would have admitted I felt bad for unleashing on the poor guy. But I wasn't at knifepoint, so I just kept going.

Halfway down the hall to the showers, out of sight of the kitchen, I heard my name again.

I froze. It was Cappy, and he'd obviously wanted me to hear. In the firehouse we didn't talk behind each other's backs, at least when it came to stuff that mattered. Sure, we would whisper a joke or two about a guy, but if it was real, we said it face-to-face. Period.

Cappy was de-escalating, trying to make it so me and Pastor Esposito could maybe one day be in the same room together again. Honestly, Cappy could have written me up for my behavior, and rightfully so, but he didn't.

"Hey, man," Cappy said to the pastor, and also to me, "Jason's a raw one. I mean, now we're gonna have to nickname him something like 'Demon Seed,' which isn't ideal for community relations, but he did kinda earn it tonight."

Pastor Esposito chuckled, and Cappy continued, "Thing is, Jason's exactly the kind of guy you want beside you in this line of work. I'd go into the pit of hell with him. And he loves helping people. It's what he lives for, but he . . ."

I could picture Cappy squinting and rubbing the back of his crew cut. It was what he did whenever he was trying to figure out what to say.

"He just doesn't have anywhere to put his pain, you know?"

I sagged against the wall and closed my eyes.

I thought about the poor kid I'd found in the closet. Before the heat and smoke took her away, what terrors had raced through her heart?

It took me back to my first day of school. I had no friends and had spent all my time with my mom up until then. I hated new situations and didn't trust strangers. Mom was my security blanket. So when I understood what "going to school" meant—spending every day away from her—I'd begged and pleaded not to go.

But she promised I'd love it. She held my hand as we walked into the classroom. We found a seat with a brightly colored name tag, and she said, "Here's where you're going to sit, honey. Isn't this fun?"

I searched for an exit. I wasn't falling for any of it. I knew that the second I sat down she would leave me with strangers, and the same thing would happen day after day. So I held tighter to her hand and tried to hide behind her leg. And then I started to cry. When the teacher pulled my mom aside into the hall for a grown-up conversation, I came along, grabbing my mom's hand like a life ring in the middle of the ocean. Maybe she would still take me home.

The teacher had other ideas. She pried my hand loose from my mom's, finger by finger, and dragged me back into class, all the while saying nice things to my mom about what a good time I'd have in class. When my mom believed the teacher, blew a kiss at me, and left, I panicked. I did everything I could to escape, but I was cornered. Hands grabbed my shirt, my arms, and I felt myself being dragged down a tiled, echoing hallway. I screamed the whole way—and when I kept screaming inside the principal's office, the grown-ups had no choice but to threaten me. To scare me into submission.

They didn't know I was already at maximum terror. The one thing I needed—my mom—was gone. I thought there was nothing scarier than that.

But then they told me about the janitor's closet. How I'd be put inside if I didn't settle down. And I was. For my own good.

The closet was pitch-dark and smelled like cleaning supplies.

"You can come out once you calm down," I heard. The voice was muffled by the door.

I came out before too long. They thought I'd calmed down. They told me I was being a good boy. I didn't tell them the real reason I'd stopped screaming. Stopped crying. I'd clammed up and froze inside that janitor's closet, not because I was good but because I didn't want to brush knees with whatever was crouched beside me in there. I could sense something cold and black, something that could wait me out. The classroom would be better. Not good, but better.

My teachers threatened me with the closet again as the years went on, but they never had to use it. Some of that darkness, that sense of overpowering hopelessness, had carved out a place inside me, and from that day on, it felt like I was carrying my own closet of fear wherever I went.

Now, as I leaned against the wall in the firehouse, I promised myself I wouldn't let the darkness overtake me again. I'd save the next victim. I would. I had to.

When enough weight had lifted from my chest that I could breathe normally again, I walked to the shower. Then I turned on the water and tried to turn off my brain.

CHAPTER 3

THE FAMILIAR DARKNESS

AS A PARAMEDIC I'D been taught something simple to tell myself on the toughest calls: it's not *my* emergency, so just deal with it.

Harsh? For sure. But in the sometimes-savage world of prehospital emergency medicine, a little inhumanity goes a long way toward saving actual humans.

As first responders, we put our own lives on the line to care for people in dire need, and often that compassion came with a necessary dose of pain. No one would describe inserting a large bore IV needle into a victim's jugular as enjoyable—especially when the victim was conscious—but if it might mean the difference between life and death, we were taught to just go for it. On one call we might need to put direct pressure on an arterial bleed caused by a broken femur protruding from the skin, and on the next call we might find ourselves shooting two hundred joules of electricity into a victim while they begged us not to. Our patients' screams guaranteed we wouldn't forget that compassion can hurt.

An old chief of mine once entered Mr. Miyagi mode when we were sitting out behind the firehouse one evening, enjoying some cigars. He said, "Jason, you leave a piece of you on every call you respond to." Wax on, wax off. "But you also pick up a piece, and it just . . . sticks with you."

I learned the truth of that on an ordinary Tuesday afternoon. We had just cleaned up lunch and were getting ready for some La-Z-Boy time when three things happened at once. The firehouse bell rang, our dot matrix printer spat out a response address, and a call from dispatch hit the firehouse speaker: "Unknown medical."

Unknown medical was a generic term our 911 dispatchers used if the call didn't fit other known categories. Our dispatchers were literal lifesavers. They could figure out a ton about a call in no time flat and relay it to us—like CPR in progress, baby not breathing, or a shooting—ensuring we'd leave the station as prepared as possible. A call for an unknown meant we'd need to figure it out on the fly. Which was good, as my preceptor had taught me—or *tried* to teach me, since ideas take a while to work their way into my skull.

Early in my career, when I was still working on an ambulance, I'd shown up to a reported headache. I'd told my partner to wait outside while I went in to give the "headache victim" some obviously needed cash for a cab ride to the hospital. But instead, when I got inside the guy was drunk, suicidal, extremely large, and holding a hand grenade. He'd been hoping a cop would respond and shoot him. I guess right about then was when I took the idea to heart that I shouldn't make assumptions on scene.

The four of us hopped on the engine and less than three minutes later rolled up to one of Oakland's ubiquitous Victorians. At least this one wasn't burning.

On medical calls me and Jimmy handled direct patient care, while

Cappy and Rog assisted as needed. Cappy still controlled the overall scene, but he never considered himself above holding a flashlight or even an IV bag for us—and he never stepped on my toes on the medical side of things. Rog would hop in and help if needed, but usually he'd be keeping a close eye on the engine to make sure none of our expensive equipment walked away, especially at night.

This time we parked right in front of the house, and the four of us walked toward it, with me and Jimmy carrying everything we might need for the unknown emergency. I had the airway bag, which was packed with every prehospital tool available to get oxygen to a patient, and Jimmy had the drug box, which was packed with forty types of IV meds, narcotics, IV bags, and more needles than the alley behind a drug house. Rog carried the monitor, the machine that let us see a victim's heart rhythm—or lack of it—and shock the heart if needed.

As I scanned the house, I made two guesses. First, the four-foot-high chain-link fence meant a dog, and second, the ramp leading to the porch meant a wheelchair or a walker. We hit the gate just as a young man appeared in the doorway. He was about my age, dressed in a plaid shirt, jeans, and white Velcro shoes. Bottle-cap glasses blurred his eyes, and he was waving what looked like a dog vest.

Why would he—

His dog, a black lab, exploded out the front door. I was a dog guy, but I was also a fireman and had taken my share of bites over the years. More often than not, the bites came from demonic lap doggies trying to protect their little old lady. But any dog is going to be on edge when large strangers show up unannounced. Based on the dog vest the young man was waving around, however, I judged we could trust this particular pup—not that we had much of a choice! I opened the front gate, and the four of us, along with our canine plus-one, raced across the dirt yard and up the ramp to the front door.

The young man immediately began waving his hands in my face and shouting unintelligibly as I stared, uncomprehending, into his hugely magnified eyes. He realized right away I didn't understand his signs or nonverbal communication—and that I probably wasn't the sharpest ax on the fire engine—so he grabbed my hand and dragged me inside.

I'd crawled through so many burning Vickies that I could navigate them blind. My new friend with limited vision and no hearing was just as capable. His dog was at heel as he pulled me through the entryway and the living room and into the kitchen. A young woman lay on her side on the checkerboard tile floor. Beside her was a chair, tipped on its side, and a Formica table. On the table was a plate with a half-eaten hamburger. There were no signs of a fight or struggle, apart from the fallen chair. I guessed the victim had either suffered a seizure or choked on her food, and that her chair had fallen over along with her.

The instant we reached the kitchen, the young man fell to his knees beside the victim. He patted the tile near her splayed hair, found a pair of glasses, and slid them back onto her face. The glasses were exactly like his. Twins, I realized. And when he began signing inches from her face, I knew they were both deaf.

I didn't understand a lick of sign language apart from thumbs-up, thumbs-down, and the good ol' middle finger, but his frantic signing and wailing cries left me in no doubt that he was trying to get his sister to wake up.

"Roll her over, Jimmy," I instructed, kneeling beside the victim. Jimmy automatically checked her breathing, then looked at me and shook his head. As I registered that information he was already feeling for a pulse.

"It's fast," he told me, "but faint."

We had work to do. She needed life-saving oxygen in her bloodstream, pronto. She also needed to unload the toxic carbon dioxide that had built up in her system. That meant we had to get her breathing. Obviously *something* had caused her to stop breathing, but it wouldn't make a difference if I found what it was before I got her breathing again. Air came first. An ambulance was on the way, so our job was to immediately begin advanced life support until it arrived.

Rog was standing at the ready next to our medical supplies in case I needed him to prep something and toss it over. Cappy was searching all the obvious places for medicine bottles, because a patient's meds could give us valuable medical history. I started right in with "the bag" from my kit, basically a balloon with a face mask attached. Once I got that going, Jimmy could take over the procedure and I could move on to figuring out why the patient wasn't breathing in the first place.

I squeezed the bag . . . nothing.

Her chest should have risen. A chest rise would let me know that fresh, oxygenated air was being properly forced into her lungs. Instead, I got nothing. I tilted her head back a bit more and squeezed the bag, and again, no chest rise. Dammit! We were dealing with a blocked airway. I could squeeze that bag with every ounce of force my 220-pound body could manage and it wouldn't make a lick of difference. Her airway was sealed up as tight as a freshly corked bottle of fine Napa wine. No air was getting through. If we couldn't get her airway open, her weak pulse was going to become no pulse, and then all the oxygen in the sky wouldn't be able to help her.

By this time Cappy had managed to get the young man back on his feet and away from his sister. Cappy was doing what he did best: keeping the scene manageable so we could do our work. Honestly, his medical chops were suboptimal, but his management skills were off the charts. He was an old-school leader. He loved to remind us that back in his day, "We were firemen, not nurses." But he was wise enough to give us our pats on the back after we saved a person's life, saying something like, "Nice going. Back in the seventies that guy would have died while we were standing around scratching our butts and waiting for the meat wagon to show up." That's usually when I'd revert to my sarcastic programming and ask him if the ambulance response times were slower then because they were pulled by horses.

Since the bag was worthless, I dropped it and grabbed my advanced airway kit, which had all the tools I needed to open the victim's lungs. I planned to put a breathing tube directly into her lungs and quickly solve the problem we were encountering. It's a tough technique for people to do in hospitals, let alone on someone's kitchen floor, but after years of doing it upside down in the rain beneath crashed cars, I had the feel of it. First step was to use my laryngoscope, which looked like a curved, dull blade attached to a handle. At the end of the blade was a small light. I would insert the blade into the victim's throat and use the light to slide the breathing tube between the vocal cords and into the lungs. And once the tube was in the lungs, I would pull the mask off the bag and attach the bag to the tube. Squeezing the bag would force the air directly into her lungs—and on the chance there was food blocking the airway, I would be able to see it and use forceps to pull it out.

Halfway through the short assembly process, I noticed the patient's lips were blue. I told Jimmy to check her pulse again.

"Bro! We lost pulse!"

I heard him fine, but I still asked, "What?"

"No pulse! No pulse!"

"Start CPR!" I barked. The girl had been alive when we arrived, and now she was clinically dead. No heartbeat, no breathing, and not much chance. We had the same cardiac medications as the hospital, but they were worthless without an airway. Oxygen had been our priority—and still was—but now we *also* had to start chest compressions. Normally with CPR you'd pause to give two breaths after every thirty chest compressions. Problem was, with the blocked airway, we couldn't give two breaths, so the compressions were just circulating blood that was already out of oxygen. It's why her heart had stopped.

With the blade ready, I yelled, "Stop CPR!"

Jimmy stopped the chest compressions so I could get a look down her throat. I inserted the laryngoscope and could finally see her airway. I blinked. But what I saw didn't change. Her airway was completely closed. No obstruction. It was swollen shut.

Jimmy began compressions again. It wasn't working, but we couldn't just sit there and chat about what to do next.

I heard hard footsteps behind me and glanced over my shoulder. An older woman had bustled into the kitchen. The young man pulled away from Cappy and crossed the tile floor. His dog went with him. The young man's hand signs were frenzied, and the older woman signed back, her hands inches from his thick glasses.

A few seconds had elapsed since I'd inserted the laryngoscope, and I was racing through our remaining treatment options when an all-too-familiar melody cut through my thoughts. The terrifying notes of a human heart breaking in real time.

"No!" the aunt or mother or caregiver screamed behind me. "No, no no, no no, no nooooo!"

I had to get that breathing tube in! I put the blade back into her mouth, tilted her head as far back as possible, and tried to force the plastic tube through the swollen flesh that was completely blocking her airway. It felt like I hit a brick wall. No matter what I did, the tube wouldn't pass through.

Behind me, Cappy was questioning the older woman. I reconstructed the story from its shattered pieces while Jimmy and I worked.

He'd cooked his sister a hamburger for lunch.

Jimmy got back on CPR compressions while I ripped open my cricothyrotomy kit.

He'd used the frying pan on the stove. The same frying pan the older woman had used the night before and forgotten to clean.

The cric kit would let me bypass the victim's mouth and upper airway altogether. I was going to have to use the surgical tools in there to punch through her cricothyroid membrane on the lower half of her neck and make a hole below the blockage above. If we could get limited airflow below the swelling, then . . .

The same frying pan the older woman had used to fry up some shrimp.

I asked Jimmy to stop CPR. Working that close to the carotid arteries while the patient's head is shaking from CPR was a bad idea. I told him to find me a good vein, because as soon as I was done with the cricothyrotomy I'd need to get an IV in.

She was deadly allergic to shellfish.

Her body had already shut down from anaphylactic shock. This wasn't some magic EpiPen scenario. I didn't carry one, since I had a way stronger dose of epinephrine in my box. If we'd arrived ten minutes earlier that medicine might have helped. But we were way past that now. If we didn't get her airway open, no drug in the world was going to help her.

"Throw a tourniquet on her arm," I told Jimmy, "and I'll feel for a vein as soon as I'm done here."

I went for it. A small bloom of red. Old air out, life-saving air in.

I sensed our ambulance crew behind me. I told the ambulance paramedic to take over the airway I had just put in. A quiet voice whispered, "No way, he did a field cricothyrotomy on her. Crazy!" I turned and saw a paramedic intern, who was riding with the two-man ambulance crew. The senior ambulance paramedic rolled his eyes. Had to be the kid's first day.

Jimmy was a superstar, but doing chest compressions is a rough workout. I yelled at the new kid to take over. I couldn't see a vein, but I could feel it under the skin and managed to get an IV line into it.

I looked away from the victim. Across the room, the young man had collapsed and was curled into a fetal position. The older woman was kneeling beside him. Her hands were beating out a regular rhythm of signs directly in front of his glasses. *Sign*, sign sign. *Sign*, sign sign.

Sign, sign sign. Her regular screams let the rest of us know exactly what she was telling him.

"*No*, you didn't kill her! *No*, you didn't kill her! *No*, you didn't kill her!"

Airway secured, IV in, CPR going, heart monitor on . . . and still flatline. Time to go. Normally the ambulance crew would be in charge of transporting the patient, including carrying the patient to the gurney out front. Not today. Me and Jimmy carried the girl out of the house and gently placed her on the gurney. I didn't want my hard-fought IV and advanced airway to be ripped out by a brand-new paramedic as he clumsily tripped his way around his first day on the job.

I watched the ambulance crew strap the seat belts on her. As they pushed the gurney to the ambulance parked behind our fire engine, I walked alongside her, continuing chest compressions. Jimmy squeezed the bag after every thirtieth compression. We were her heart and lungs, and she desperately needed us working for her. We would often pass off our calls to the ambulance medics when they arrived, but on major traumas or medicals I liked to ride along to give continuity of care.

Door closed. Siren on. We were on the move. I was giving her a load of IV cardiac meds, along with another set of medications to help with the anaphylaxis induced by the shrimp allergy. But her heart wasn't responding.

The ambulance shook as we cornered, accelerated, braked, and accelerated. The ambulance paramedic and his intern handled the CPR while I watched the monitors that were now attached to her. They all showed death. I also watched the time. Every three minutes I would administer another dose of IV medication.

I was totally checked in to the patient care I was doing, but my mind was checking out. We took pride in leaving each scene we responded to in better condition than the way we found it when we arrived. We usually accomplished this by making people better, but erasing a bit of the trauma from the place mattered too. Of course, we always gathered the medical trash of our trade—IV bag wrappers, torn med boxes, used bags and needles—but we went beyond that. Our goal was to make the room appear as if no medical emergency had occurred.

I could picture Cappy, Jimmy, and Rog back at the house. Right then I knew they were stuffing the half-eaten hamburger into one of their trash bags, washing the plate, picking up the chair, and straightening up.

And I pictured the older woman pulling the young man toward her car, helping him buckle in, and racing to the hospital. I wondered if she could sign while she drove.

As soon as we dropped off the victim at the ER, I gave a verbal report to the doctor and the team taking over patient care and jotted down all the medications we had given her to the nurse for documentation.

Then I heard the doc say, "And the time of death is . . ."

All the work we had been doing was finished. She was gone.

"Hey, fire guy," the doc asked, "did you do that cric?"

I nodded.

"Strong work. You guys did good. But sometimes . . ."

I was already walking toward the exit, ignoring his kudos. In two recent shifts I'd let four people die. Normally, whether someone survived or died, I never wanted to hang around the hospital. I never wanted to know. My job was to give a victim a chance. And then give the next victim a chance. And the victim after that. It was a treadmill. It was also the life I'd chosen, and I couldn't imagine doing anything else. But that time I did something I never did. I felt an urge to turn around and look back.

I immediately regretted my decision. The older woman had arrived with the young man, and they were shoulder to shoulder near where I'd left his sister. His dog was standing beside him. The old woman was still signing, her fingers flying near his eyes. Then I saw him look down, choosing not to see what the older woman was signing, and shake his head. I saw him fall onto his knees. I saw him bury his head in the neck of his service dog. I saw his shoulders heaving. I saw the older woman stop signing and cover her face in her hands.

I felt like an invader. The scene blurred as my eyes filled with tears.

Outside, Cappy, Jimmy, and Rog rolled up. No words were exchanged as I climbed aboard our engine. I'd be back at the fire-house in a few minutes, and when my shift ended in eighteen hours, I'd head back home.

Home. The word felt almost like a curse, or a mockery of my pain. What was I supposed to tell myself? It's not *my* emergency, so just deal with it? But what if someone else's emergency became mine? What if I collected so many painful pieces on so many calls that I was no longer me?

I'd failed. Again. And I had no one to walk through it with me.

The familiar darkness descended. It wasn't welcome, but it was becoming the only thing I understood.

CHAPTER 4
DAY OFF

AT OAKLAND FIRE, WE worked one on, two off. I was required to be at my firehouse for a single twenty-four-hour shift—0800 hours to 0800 hours—and then spend forty-eight hours recuperating at home.

On the one hand, every time I drove to work it was my Friday. Most people envied that, but for me, it was a worse deal than it sounded. Work was pretty much the only place I wanted to be, because it was the only place I didn't have to think. Between shifts I had way too much time on my hands and stress on my mind. More downtime meant more time to relive the emotions of my previous shift—and no shift was ever chill.

I felt the highest level of respect for my brothers and sisters fighting fire in slower areas across our great country. Their structures burned just as hot, their domestic calls were just as dangerous, and their medical emergencies came with the same level of severe suck attached to them. The one difference was frequency. Bad wires, unattended food left on the stove, a burning candle . . . a fire could ignite anywhere.

And brokenness and evil were everywhere because *people* were everywhere. In Oakland, though, just like in any other compact urban area, the odds that something would go wrong were just way higher. And when a spark hit somewhere as literally and figuratively combustible as Oakland, well, it tended to light up a whole lot of folks.

The intensity of my work shifts was why I was so protective about my commute. I'd always hang around a few minutes after my shift ended, hoping for some overtime. Staying at work was way better than being forced to go home. But since I was forced to take my required time off, I figured I might as well get as much rest and do as little thinking as possible. And getting in the right headspace began with the sixty-mile drive between Oakland and my house in Santa Rosa.

Eddie, one of my bros who worked a different shift at the firehouse, regularly burned me custom CDs with music he got from some mysterious source. I never asked how he did it, and he never asked what in the world I was thinking with my random requests. He'd just read my list of bands, shake his head, and then a few days later I'd have a disc waiting for me, usually with something like "Demon Seed's Dumb-Ass Mix #9" scrawled on it with a Sharpie.

It had been eighteen hours—filled with a car fire and seven additional medical calls—since walking away from the boy and his dog in the ER, but I still couldn't get the scene out of my head. I fired up my Toyota Tacoma and slotted my latest mix in the CD player. This time I'd requested a few classics from Johnny Cash, followed by my girl Gwen Stefani belting it out with No Doubt. From there the music shifted gears to Metallica before ending with the soothing crooning of Simon & Garfunkel. I wanted to create the right vibe of, well, mindlessness, and I'd try to ride that vibe through my hour-long commute and my two days off.

I knew guys from OFD who'd been smart enough (or old enough) to grab houses in Oakland when real estate was still within reach of a firefighter's salary. But beginning sometime in the 1990s, a guy like me would need an OFD salary plus a million bucks under the mattress to make things work in the city proper. Most of my peers and I preferred to get more bang for our buck by living farther away. An hour's drive a couple times a week was no big deal for me, and it meant I could have a real house rather than a tiny apartment in the city where I'd fall asleep to the soothing sounds of gunshots and guard dogs barking all night long.

My route was automatic. North out of Oakland, across San Francisco Bay on the Richmond Bridge, then up US Route 101 through San Rafael and Petaluma. As I transitioned from the inner city to the Sonoma County wine country, it should have been refreshing to see the razor wire that surrounded the tops of security fences in Oakland turn into barbed wire that kept cows within their pastures. But today my ride felt wrong somehow. Gwen and the fellas weren't doing anything to lighten my mood, and my truck felt like it was pushing through sludge. Everything felt heavier. Slower. I'd be staring at the highway and—*blink*—all of a sudden I'd be looking at one of the recent victims I'd failed to save or one of the grieving, broken survivors I'd had to walk away from.

I wasn't the only first responder to have trouble shaking the people I'd lost. That was part of any firefighter's job. Difference was, the victims had never kept me company on my drive home. I also wasn't the only one who craved the adrenaline of the job as a way to escape pain, loneliness, or loss. Wanting to stay at work wasn't that uncommon. But it seemed my never wanting to be alone was a few steps past normal.

I pulled into an old truck stop in Petaluma to fill up the tank. They had the cheapest gas, and the bathrooms were so dirty that if I was on my way to work and needed to throw up after a night of drinking, no one would care.

When I was ready to go, I turned on the ignition, and it hit me. *I've got a black hole inside me.*

As soon as the thought hit my brain, I knew it was undeniably true. It was like one of those things you can't unsee.

I'd been walking in darkness all my life. It was the only thing I knew as a kid. In school. At home. Every waking moment of my life sucked. If I wasn't getting yelled at, I was being ignored. If I wasn't feeling terrorized, I was depressed or angry. Growing up hadn't changed a thing. I had a house, a job, an identity, and still the darkness covered everything I did. Everything I felt. But now it was like all that darkness had collapsed and was inside me.

I turned the truth over and over in my brain so I could see it from all angles. My black hole was small at least. I mean, small enough that I was still functioning. I could still drive and eat and go to work and seem normal to the guys at the firehouse. But a black hole was a black hole, no matter the size. Every scrap of happiness I managed to grab would eventually be sucked into that black hole, never to see the light of day. Worse, I suspected my black hole was gaining size. The one thing that had always kept me stable was saving people, but my black hole was beginning to pull in even that. And if it was consuming more and more of my life, I realized, eventually it would consume me.

I skipped back to Metallica, turned up the volume, and punched the accelerator.

The house I owned in Santa Rosa was a 902-square-foot middle finger to the shame of my childhood.

The edged and mowed grass, the window-box planters filled with blooming geraniums, the fire-engine red front door with a polished brass door knocker, the row of comfortable chairs on the porch for when the guys stopped by, all of it was my way of proving I was better than the small, dirty one-story duplex me and Dad moved into after the divorce. The polished oak floors inside helped me forget the stained carpet of my childhood. The original 1950s kitchen was spotless and gleaming, pushing away the anxiety that gripped me whenever I remembered my continual failure to keep the duplex clean enough while Dad was at work. My queen pillow-top mattress, Amish sleigh bed frame, and eight-hundred-thread-count sheets covered over my memories of a sagging mattress and a room decorated with nothing besides piles of dirty clothes.

"Bro, know what your place looks like?" Jimmy had asked me once as several of us drank beers on my porch. "It looks like Martha Stewart threw up all over it!"

Before I could respond, Chad, a friend from San Francisco Fire I'd met a few years before, jumped in. "Hey, don't worry. Jimmy means that as a compliment." He waited exactly the right amount of time before adding, "*Martha.*"

Embracing that part of my life had always been one of my best coping mechanisms, despite how at odds it seemed with my bachelor firefighter image. Two days of enforced rest passed quicker when I was pulling tiny weeds out of my blue fescue lawn or repainting the wall in my living room with an offsetting color for the seventh time in a year.

As I rolled up to the curb outside my house, I tried to create a mental to-do list. I knew forcing myself to stay awake for the next twelve hours was going to be rough. But keeping a regular sleep schedule at home was the only way to guarantee I'd be alert at work. If I fell asleep right when I got home, it would usually mean staying awake all night and showing up to a shift already half-tired. So I had twelve hours of daylight I needed to somehow fill, when all I wanted to do was nothing. Absolutely nothing.

I wandered inside and opened my fridge. It looked like it always did: two quarts of milk, a pack of lunch meat, and some condiment bottles. The kitchen was spotless. I'd just cleaned it two days earlier. I wandered into the hall, the living room, the bedroom, and the bathroom. Pristine, all of it. Back yard, garage, front yard . . . I couldn't find a single thing to keep me busy.

Maybe a run will pass the time. The idea stopped me mid-stride in the front yard. *A run?* Things were going from bad to worse in my head if I was coming up with ideas like that. I wasn't one of those guys who enjoyed running, or even pretended to. I actively disliked running—and so did my flat feet. Firemen didn't save many people by running three miles. That was why the internal combustion engine had been invented. But since I had to pass the time until dark somehow, I grabbed my keys from the hall table inside and locked the front door. Still wearing my OFD T-shirt, blue shorts, and Nikes, I hopped back in my truck and headed out.

Santa Rosa and Oakland felt like they should be in *A Tale of Two Cities.* Not that I'd ever read that book. In fact, since first grade I'd only managed to read cover to cover *Tales of a Fourth Grade Nothing,* plus my EMT manual and some old *Reader's Digest* magazines the previous owners of my house had left behind in a box.

Santa Rosa was smaller than Oakland, yeah, but it wasn't *that* small. Yet it seemed like it was located on another planet. I cruised through the historic downtown. It was a beautiful mess of brick storefronts, well-kept Victorians, train tracks, and flourishing businesses. Where there would have been a homeless encampment in Oakland, Santa Rosa had a park with a fountain. Turn-of-the-century buildings had been turned into wine bars, hip coffee shops, and microbreweries instead of standing as burned-out shells. Seven nights a week, the bars in Santa Rosa were packed to the gills with college kids from Sonoma State and the local community college. If there was a local recycling program, I'd never noticed it. In Oakland, you couldn't miss the army of hungry people pushing shopping carts full of cans and bottles to the collection center.

Living within stumbling distance of the local bar scene should have been perfect for a young firefighter. I'd spent my share of nights yelling at the ball game with my buddies while scarfing down wings and beer or dropping well-placed hints about fighting fire to the cute blonde, brunette, or redhead beside me. But all of it was just me killing time. I wasn't a fan of any sports, and I didn't really want a relationship with any of the girls I dated. I was just going through the motions, hoping somehow a spark might ignite within me and I could start feeling the same happiness as the people surrounding me who were doing the same things. I wanted to trade in my fake pleasures for real pleasure, but so far *so not* good.

I left downtown and headed for Annadel State Park. That open space was the closest thing I had to a church. I wasn't one of those new age types who worshipped trees, but there was something about that place that centered me. There was a particular smell, a mixture of California oak, dry grass, and the occasional redwood. One of the trails led to a small lake, and another one to a hillside that felt like it overlooked all of creation. Being in Annadel State Park was usually as close as I could come to being at peace.

When I had to run for whatever reason, I always ran according to my personal SLOW method. It was perfect for people who hated running, had the attention span of a squirrel, and had the misfortune of being able to picture the bodies of victims whenever they stood still for too long. It was the way I cleared my head, literally. Working that hard put me on the ragged edge of oxygen debt, with no room for contemplation.

*S*tart out hard.

*L*ower for push-ups.

*O*n your feet and go again.

*W*ait for the burning.

And then repeat until you get to the top, pass out, or puke.

I parked near the lake, where kids were tossing bread crumbs to the ducks as their moms complained about teachers, husbands, and other moms who weren't there. But right away the trail ascended in switchbacks through the oaks and pines, and I pretty much had the place to myself. When I hit the top I stopped, fingers laced on top of my head as I tried to open my lungs wide. My breathing slowed. Sweat dripped from my hair and face. My vision sharpened. I glanced inside my head, hoping to see that I'd been reset—my switch flipped from emergency Jason to plain old Jason.

Instead, I saw my black hole.

It pulsed and grew a fraction larger. It had just consumed my attempt to deal with my darkness and wanted to know what was next on the menu.

On the outside I looked like any other carefree jogger in the park. On the inside I was devastated, shaking a mental fist at the heavens. *What the hell?! I'm burning through ways to deal with life real fast here, universe. If surviving is up to me, you're making things impossible.*

I'd always worked out my problems myself. I never asked anyone to carry what I could carry on my own. So sharing my pain with anyone was out of the question. I knew that if I did, I might create a bond with someone—which my black hole would inevitably consume. Usually, in uncomfortable social situations, I would control the conversation to protect myself. Unfortunately, my current conversation was with something inside of me. Something bigger than me. Something I couldn't control any more than I could explain it away.

As I stood there in Annadel State Park, I felt truly alone. Terrified. *Just make it to bedtime*, I told myself.

I sat calmly on my couch, staring at the television.

Bang, bang, bang.

We had a way of knocking that let people know it was a *fireman* knocking. It was less "knock, knock, who's there?" and more "knock, knock, we're coming in whether you like it or not."

Bang, bang, bang, bang, bang.

I sighed. The guys didn't know for sure I was inside. My truck was at the curb, but for all they knew I was out for a jog or already downtown at one of our favorite bars, cruising for a phone number or a free shot. I knew they would pound on my door for a few minutes and then leave. My beloved pack of clowns would get back in their clown car and go make merry without me. They were nice enough to want me along, but they certainly didn't need me. And I felt incapable of needing them or anyone else. What was the point? My black hole was ready and willing to devour absolutely anything—and, like me, it was ready to respond on a moment's notice.

Alcohol. Weekends waterskiing at the lake. Fighting fire. Rescuing people. Respect. Every single thing I wanted or tried to want or wanted to want to want would end up in the same place eventually.

I'd spent almost my entire life perfecting my body language so no one could tell what I was thinking from how I was acting. If someone looked through my living room window, they would have seen a typical guy relaxing on the couch and watching television.

Except my television was unplugged, just like it always was.

I couldn't take my eyes off the screen. I stared at it, willing my brain to unplug, to turn off and become blank and featureless. Sadly for me, my brain still had energy. And after watching that kid and his service dog in the ER, of course, my brain thought of Bandit.

Mom had bought an Airedale terrier for me when I was in fourth grade and told me Bandit could live with me at Dad's place. But Dad didn't like having a dog inside the house almost as much as he didn't like the fact that my mom had sent the dog to his place without asking. After two long nights of watching Bandit shiver in the cold rain outside, I built her a doghouse in the side yard. I found scraps of wood around the neighborhood and dragged them home, eventually cobbling together something like a dog shack. It had three walls and a roof, plus my oldest blanket for Bandit to sleep on.

For the first time I looked forward to something every day. After I walked home from school, I'd go straight to the side yard and kneel, and Bandit would put her paws up on me, tail wagging a million miles an hour. For a few minutes everything was perfect. She didn't know any tricks, but she knew how to love, and that was good enough for me.

Over time, my dad came up with reasons why Bandit had to go. He said she was destroying the yard, even though the yard had been junky long before she arrived. He claimed she was too loud and that he didn't want to keep spending money on her food. I would have fed her my own food, but that wasn't an option.

Then came the day he told me he was putting an ad in the newspaper: "Dog. Free to Good Home."

I held Bandit in my lap the entire ride to her new home, sobbing silently. I tried to say goodbye, but I knew it was a one-way conversation. She snuggled me like she always did, having no idea what was about to happen. All too soon we were at the "Good Home."

"Goodbye, girl," I whispered into her fur.

Dad parked but left the truck running. He took Bandit from my lap and walked her to the front door. I watched through the window long enough to see her turn her head back. She was still looking back at me as she trotted into the strange front door, which closed behind her.

The memory faded. Outside my perfect little house, the sun sank, painting my living room orange and pink.

I hoped sleep would turn my brain off. But what then?

I'd worry about making it through tomorrow tomorrow.

CHAPTER 5

APARTMENT #312

ME, JIMMY, ROG, AND Cappy scattered across our local Pak 'N Save, grabbing the items off our shopping list.

We were currently without any rookies at the station to bring us fresh donuts and brew our coffee, so we'd defaulted to lazy and chowed down on leftovers from the previous shift's dinner while doing our housework and equipment checks. Breakfast might have been bachelor city, but lunch and dinner were always on a different level. We split the cost, the cooking, and the cleanup, and we always ate together. Period. No exceptions. Sharing two meals a day glued our little community together as tightly as responding to emergencies did.

Since it was Saturday, we were going all out. On weekends we did an 11:00 a.m. brunch: eggs over easy, fried potatoes, bacon, sausage, and pancakes, washed down with orange juice. Then for dinner we'd chow down on our world-famous steak and Caesar: a perfectly grilled rib eye—which meant still mooing for most of us—a piping-hot baked potato with butter, chives, and sour cream, and our Caesar salad with from-scratch *everything*, down to the croutons. Our firehouse had its own recipe that was never written down, and we'd pass it on to the younger guys only when they were ready for that level of responsibility.

I was chatting up the butcher at the Pak 'N Save when a call squawked on my belt radio: "Engine eleven, you are needed for an unknown medical." The dispatcher continued with the address and cross street. It was just a couple of blocks away.

The four of us ditched our carts and ran to our fire engine parked in the red zone outside. The store employees knew us and always rolled our carts into the dairy fridge until we came back.

I knew the apartment complex we were going to from countless previous calls, and I sized it up mentally during our quick ride. It was a three-story brick job, built in the 1920s. It used to be a hotel, but some rich slumlord bought it and was making good income from the Section 8 money he was pocketing, while neglecting proper upkeep for the old building.

When we pulled on scene, it looked just as I had remembered, except worse. More broken windows, more trash. Some cars that had been up on blocks were now sitting right on the ground wheel-less, and one was even flipped over. The building had twenty units per floor, and as we climbed the interior stairwell and walked toward the apartment, I took mental note of the layout. I had no doubt we'd be returning to this building, except then we'd be advancing a hose line in pitch darkness.

The door to #312 opened, but only as wide as the security chain allowed. The interior of the apartment looked to be pitch-dark. I couldn't make out the occupant beyond a wrist gripping the doorknob and a pair of gleaming eyes.

"Come in," said the voice on the other side of the door.

The female voice sounded weak. Young-weak and scared-weak for sure, and maybe some other kind as well. The door closed, and I heard the chain being undone. Then the door opened a few inches and remained there. I frowned, waited a few seconds, put my gloved hand on the door, and pushed. The door swung open all the way. Daylight poured in across a filthy linoleum floor. The four of us stepped inside, and Cappy eased the door shut behind him.

I blinked at the sudden changes in brightness. Only a tiny fraction of the bright sun outside reached the dark kitchen where we stood. The one window in view had a piece of cardboard taped across it, and morning light leaked around the cardboard like blood around a bandage. A candle burned on a small table—never a good thing from a firefighter's point of view—and in its trembling light I saw the woman who had opened the door. She was sitting at the table, illuminated by the flame. My heart fell. Even without being able to see the rest of the dark apartment, I made some educated guesses about what we'd find. I'd been inside enough places like this in my city to last a lifetime.

Hell, I'd grown up in a place like this.

I heard Cappy click on his flashlight behind me. I knew he'd check out the rest of the apartment. I shoved down my feelings and got to work. The woman was sobbing silently, and I stepped toward her and took a knee.

"How are you?" I asked. My smile was probably the brightest thing in the room.

She shrugged and looked at the floor. The candlelight made her tears look painted on. She couldn't have been much older than twenty-five. After a few seconds she looked back at me, like she was checking to see if I was going to stay with her.

"I'm sick," she began, "and . . . and . . ."

I nodded like she'd told me everything I needed to know. And in a way she had. Here was a single woman's struggle, repeated way too many times across Oakland. I could tell she was worn out, broken down, and just plain tired. Bone tired. Of every single thing in her life.

I could relate.

On calls like this I never tried to puzzle out the whys and hows that led to someone calling the fire department for a nonemergency.

All I could do was try to figure out how to make it better. Yeah, she had what appeared to be the flu, but it wasn't severe enough to call for an $800 ride to the hospital. Cappy radioed the dispatch to cancel the ambulance that had been responding with us. My educated guess was that her flu had just intensified all the other issues that were kicking her down.

Feeling bad sucks for anyone. But when that person feels like they have zero options, well . . . feeling bad becomes despair real quick.

I moved step by step through a full medical assessment. She was slightly malnourished and dehydrated. But not to the level of needing an IV. She just needed to drink a little more water and eat. I heard the professional whispers between Cappy and the guys, confirming what I already knew. No electricity. And after hearing the squeak of the cabinets opening and closing and getting a whiff of the stench that came out of her warm refrigerator, I could guess what had led her to call the fire department. She'd probably been awake all night, desperately going through her options—family, neighbors, church, exes—and found not one person she could turn to for help. When she'd truly run out of options and felt completely alone, she'd picked up her dying cell phone and dialed 911.

What did it say about this woman that literally the only person she could ask for help was a stranger on the other end of an emergency line? What did it say about our city? About me?

All this was running through my mind as I finished taking her blood pressure, when something caught my attention. Previously, Cappy had been holding his hand over his flashlight beam to keep the light soft. He had just removed his hand and aimed the powerful beam toward the farthest edge of the room. Suddenly the inky shadows behind the woman resolved into the shape of two queen mattresses pushed together on the floor and covered in piles of blankets.

I looked more closely, and one of the blankets sat up. As the blanket fell away, I saw a girl who looked about ten years old.

Cappy quickly shielded his flashlight beam and stepped as quietly as he could toward the mattresses. When he turned back to look at me, he held up five fingers, then one finger, and did a rock-the-baby motion with his arms.

Five children sleeping on the floor. Five siblings huddled together for warmth. And the youngest was only a baby. Now the woman's desperation made perfect sense.

I sorted the situation into concentric circles of danger. Getting rid of the burning candle was priority one. I'd seen far too much destruction of property and life caused by candles just like this one. That meant we'd need to get her electricity back on. Next was food. And after that . . . well, we'd just have to wing it. There was no point in calling Child Protective Services. If we called every time we rolled up to a situation like this, the system would be swamped. We saved our calls for the people doing *actual* bad things to kids. When it came to families who were stuck in a cycle, we just tried to help.

I put the candle out with the pinch of two fingers and dropped it in my pocket. I wasn't stealing it—it was more like a trade for some other goods. As much as I wanted to remove the cardboard over her window and introduce the beautiful Bay Area morning to her, I didn't. She obviously wasn't ready to let the light shine in just yet. I respected that.

Pain comes in far too many varieties. This woman was suffering a unique type: asking a complete stranger for help, knowing she could be refused or even penalized. We weren't going to let that happen.

Jimmy had been on his cell phone in the kitchen. He came to my side and spoke softly to the woman. "Ma'am, you oughta have a few months of electricity now," he told her, "but the billing department is gonna get wise before too long and disconnect you if you can't pay." It was an old trick of ours to notify the electric company of a "life safety issue."

The woman's crying kicked up a notch.

I saw Rog exit the front door. "Rog is gonna run down to the Kwik-E-Mart," I explained, "and grab a few things."

Those places were on every other corner, and despite being called *markets* they mostly peddled junk food, lottery tickets, cigarettes, and dirt-cheap liquor. Still, calories from Twinkies, a gallon of milk, and a few bags of chips were a lot better than zero. I knew Rog would do his best to find a few days' worth of food we could stash in the kitchen, hopefully before the rest of the kids woke up. In situations like this, we always wanted the kids to think their mom or dad had provided for them, not some strangers wearing funny clothes. We made more money than most of the people we served, so there was an unspoken rule to give back whenever we could make a difference.

Other than some electricity, food, social service referrals, and a bit of cash, there was absolutely nothing else we could do. That night the kids would still be sharing two filthy mattresses on the floor. The next morning a scared, powerless mother would still wake up feeling like she might not be able to make it through the day.

Rog reentered the apartment with several full plastic bags. He set them on the counter and nodded at Cappy. Cappy smiled at the woman and told her, "Good luck, ma'am. We've gotta get back in service for our next call."

She stood and wrapped her arms around each of us in turn. When she reached me, I was surprised by the intensity of her hug. "Why are you doing this?" she sobbed. I could feel her whole body shaking.

Maybe it was a good question from her point of view. No one else in her life had stepped up when she needed help—or more likely, she didn't *have* anyone else in her life. But for us it was never a question. We couldn't *not* help her. We served our city and the people in it. Period. Rich or poor, old or young, literally burning to death or literally starving to death. Bottom line: it was the right thing to do.

I squeezed her back. "Our job's to help," I said into the top of her hair. "Just to help, not to judge."

CHAPTER 6

MR. WEI'S DONUTS AND CHINESE CUISINE

SEEMED LIKE MORE AND more of my nights were sleepless.

I rolled over for the thousandth time and checked my alarm clock: 4:00 a.m. *You're screwed, Sautel.* Yep. With zero sleep under my belt, I climbed out of bed, hopped into some clothes, and headed off to work.

Technically our shift began at 8:00 a.m., but most guys showed up early to relieve the off-going crew. When you were beat up and beat down after a hard shift, getting a head start toward home made a big difference, whether by grabbing an extra hour of sleep or helping your spouse get the kids off to school.

I often showed up *real* early. I liked the camaraderie of the firehouse as much as I hated being alone at home. I never shared details about my personal struggles with the guys at the station, but Cappy understood people as much as he understood fire. It was part of what made him great at his job. Once he'd said to me, "Hey, kid, you aren't on probation anymore. You don't have to be the first guy here every morning." When I told him it just felt better to be at work than at home, he never brought it up again.

I knew our off-going crew would love to wake up to donuts and coffee, so I took a short detour to my favorite place. Mr. Wei's Donuts and Chinese Cuisine was a donut shop in the morning, but come lunchtime it transitioned into a traditional Chinese take-out restaurant. The donuts always had a hint of egg roll taste, and in return, the egg rolls had a hint of a donut flavor—but for some strange reason it worked, and the guys loved them.

I tossed three pink boxes on the front seat of my truck and drove the half mile to our station. The streets were trapped in a limbo between times. Virtually everyone who worked nine-to-five jobs was just waking up. And people who had maybe less respectable ideas the night before—like hitting a strip club until 2:00 a.m. closedown— were still in bed. The only ones wandering the streets of Oakland in the wee hours of the morning were people like me: the hurt and the lost. The difference was that I was privileged enough to have a good job, a bed of my own, and a place to shower. But I figured we were the same kind of broken.

We firefighters knew this time all too well. We understood and served the addicted who wandered the night like zombies, looking for that elusive morsel of crack cocaine in back alleys, gutters, and abandoned houses. We knew them by name, like Joe, who preferred to be called Moe. Or Shirley, who always grinned ear to ear and yelled, "There goes my boys. Be careful, babies!" as we passed her cardboard encampment on the way to our next fire. Or "the mayor," who was the most senior resident of the tent park that backed up against the on-ramp to Interstate 880.

These folks were dismissed by almost everyone. But to us, they were just some of the people we served, and we loved doing it. Still, the sounds of that time in the morning were like sad notes fading into daylight. Fist fights and cursing. Moaning. The shuffle of ratty shoes or bare feet or hands and knees on sidewalks. Shopping carts filled with metal junk being pushed nowhere in particular. Stray dogs—we affectionately called them ghetto deer—rummaging through whatever garbage the homeless folks pulled out of the dumpsters as they looked for treasures to take to the recycling center.

In short, the only ones on the streets were *those people*.

I'd heard that phrase way too many times, usually uttered like a curse. Sure, they were around during the day as well, but at predawn, they were the only ones around. It sucks to live under a system that seems to keep *you* from having access to the stuff everyone *else* has. There's no physical wall between the upscale neighborhoods of the Oakland hills and the flatlands of Oakland, but there is an invisible one. You can feel it, see it, and sense it in so many different ways. Dads tell their kids to roll up the car windows on their leather-seated sedans. Moms anxiously ask how long it will take to get back on the freeway.

The guys at our firehouse drove back and forth through that wall on every shift. Not many of us lived in Oakland, but we served there, and that was what mattered. We understood.

Politics was politics. In my experience, both sides talked out the sides of their mouths, at least when it came to the folks we served in Oakland. Some bigwig with a tie and a hard hat would show up, usually with a security detail, for a photo op in front of an empty lot or a burned-down Victorian and say things like "economic investment and redevelopment" or "thriving community that's stronger together." Then all that nice talk would be forgotten the moment they started mingling with their own folks in the halls of power.

Our neighborhood felt like a lost cause filled with lost people.

Castoffs, castaways, and throwaways.

Maybe that's why I enjoyed helping them so much. I was as hopeless as they were.

—◇—

I pulled up to the back gate of the firehouse and left my truck running. It was still dark enough that I needed my headlights angled toward the gate so I could read the combination lock. Once I opened it, I'd park in our secure lot and relock the gate.

Back near the beginning of my career, when I was much younger and the same amount of dumb, an instructor had taught me to keep my head on a swivel. By *taught* I mean he told me to keep my head on a swivel, and a few seconds later he slapped me upside the head to demonstrate both the necessity of doing so and my lack of skill in following his directions. It was good advice, and I never forgot it. There were a lot of broken-down folks in the neighborhood we served. Not that everyone was dangerous, far from it, but it would have been naive (or worse) to pretend everyone was a model citizen.

I squinted at the lock and moved my body to one side, hoping to get a bit more light. *Seventeen. Fifty-two.* From behind me I heard the metallic rattle of a shopping cart. Considering my truck was idling, the fact that I could hear the shopping cart behind me meant its owner was already uncomfortably close.

I eased upright and turned around casually, stepping out of the glare of my truck's headlights. I let my arms hang loose at my sides and shifted my weight onto my back foot just in case. I spotted him. He was an older gentleman, pushing a cart filled with what looked like scrap metal and arguing with someone.

Several someones, actually—and they were all invisible. The old man was telling someone to leave him alone and asking someone else for help. He was also repeating, "Leave me alone, leave me alone," followed by, "I'm sorry, please, please."

Over the years I'd learned how to size up a person almost instantly. And I was almost never wrong. I could tell the shopping-cart guy was harmless. He'd pass me right by, lost in his own inner struggle. It was unfortunate, but he'd have to battle his own demons today.

As he wandered closer, I could tell he was tall, despite his hunched shoulders and curved back. If he stood up straight he'd be a few inches past six feet, and the hands wrapped around the shopping cart looked strong enough to crush my big head like a grape. He was clean-shaven, which pegged him as a shelter user who lived on the streets but still had access to a razor and a sink.

I planned to just stand in the twilight and let him trundle on down the alley before I finished unlocking the gate.

He continued to talk to the imaginary people, but quieter. He knew I was close, and I could tell he was trying to act normal and not scare me. It saddened me because he looked ashamed. I guessed he was muffling his voice because he didn't want me judging or clowning him for trying his best to deal with his reality.

He was even with the front of my truck when all of a sudden he stopped and stared into the cab through the open door.

I frowned at him.

He smiled, but not at me.

Then I tracked his eyes. The pink donut boxes.

The old man turned toward me and asked, "Can I have one?" His words were soft and gentle-sounding. The other voices in his head must have been drowned out by the siren call of Mr. Wei's donuts.

I grinned at him and said, "Oh, *heck* yeah!"

I stepped to the combo lock and respun it, then came around to the cab of the truck. The man had let go of his cart and stood expectantly.

"Hey, man, which ones are your favorites?" I asked. I pulled open the top of the closest box and a wave of warm, sugared air wafted out.

With an index finger more crooked than a politician, he pointed at the biggest donut in the box.

I laughed. "Dude, apple fritters are my favorite too," I said, pulling out two. I looked over my shoulder and saw that the lights inside the firehouse were still off. There was no rush.

"Come on back," I invited, switching off the ignition, "and we can take a load off."

I opened my tailgate, and we hopped up, side by side. It made a perfect spot to sit and relax. When I handed him his apple fritter, he looked me in the eyes and said, "Thank you very much, sir."

I quickly looked away from his face. He wore a blue work shirt with at least two other shirts layered beneath it. Nodding toward the oval name tag stitched onto his work shirt, I asked, "Guessing your name isn't Suzanne?"

He laughed. "Nope!"

He took off his beret and ran his fingers across his bald head. I tried to look more closely at his beret, thinking it could be army issue, but he replaced it before I could be sure.

After a minute or two of silently enjoying the sweet taste of those fritters, I decided to spark up a conversation. Seeing as he might be a military man, I opened with the universal language spoken and understood by all blue-collar workers: humor.

"On your way to work?" I asked.

He almost spit his donut out when he laughed. "Man, that's why I have mad respect for you firemen. Y'all are legit." He took another bite and continued, "Yeah, man, I'm on my way to work," and then he chuckled again.

I laughed back. "Me too!" I said. "What a coincidence!"

That's when it hit me that the argument he'd been having with everyone in his head was over. It was just him and me enjoying each other's company.

"Tell me something, fireman," he said, taking another bite and looking off toward the silhouettes of the high-rises downtown. "You *like* being a fireman?"

The answer I gave surprised me, because I'd never shared it with anyone. "It's a good job. Helping people in their time of need, alongside your brothers. That doesn't feel like work, you know?"

He nodded.

"Working here," I continued, waving my donut at the dark city around us, "feels more like a calling or something. A community. I grew up feeling like an outcast. When I was seven or eight, my mom moved across the state. My dad was a Vietnam vet. He didn't teach me a whole lot of positives when it came to relationships. Feels like the first eighteen years of my life I just bounced from one failure to the next. So now, being a fireman is part of what's keeping me alive. When I'm not at the firehouse I feel dead inside."

I paused. The homeless man continued to eat his donut beside me.

"I guess what I'm saying is, being lonely sucks." I looked at him. "But here, at the firehouse, the loneliness doesn't suck quite as much. Does that make any sense?"

He replied with the most honest answer possible. "I get it," he said. "And, fireman? Vietnam and coming home . . . that was tough. I know your old man was rough on you, but life was rough on him too."

He went on to tell me about how he'd been raised, what the war had been like for him, how he'd lost everything because of mental illness, and how all he could think about was finding enough alcohol each day to help him forget his mental illness, the war, and his childhood.

And then we just sat in the dark, eating another round of Mr. Wei's finest. I couldn't guess what he was thinking, but I was thinking how alike we were, side by side on the tailgate of my truck.

When the first light popped on in the firehouse, I wiped my sticky fingers on my pants. "Listen, man, I gotta get to work," I told him, "but it's been good chatting with you. Really good."

Both of us hopped down, and I gave him an extra donut for the road. He returned to his shopping cart, but instead of moving on he placed one hand over his heart and said, "Thank you." He said it so softly it was hard to hear. "Thank you for *blessing* me."

Whatever I'd been expecting him to say, it hadn't been that. One, I had no idea what he meant. Two, even if I took a stab at his meaning, it didn't seem like it applied to me. *Bless* was a religious word. A good word. Whatever else I was, I wasn't a blesser.

"Enjoy the donut," I said. It was all I could think to say. I regretted the words the second they came out of my mouth. What was I, working the counter at Mr. Wei's?

The man smiled at me, then took hold of his cart and began to push it down the alley. Not ten steps in he began yelling at imaginary people—or as I now understood, real figures who existed only in his memory.

I watched him leave, wishing I didn't understand him as well as I did.

—◇—

Inside the firehouse, I unstacked and opened the donut boxes on the kitchen table, then set the first pot of coffee brewing.

I knew from experience what was happening in the dorm across the apparatus hall. It was just like in those old cartoons where the semitransparent fingers of a delicious smell lift a character up from his bed and drag him toward the source. My slumbering giants tucked in twenty feet away were starting to move around in their bunks. The first fingers of scent were tickling their nostrils. I folded my arms and leaned against the wall to watch.

The first guy lumbered through the kitchen door. It was Benny. He'd been on the job for thirty years and liked to keep everyone posted—loudly—on his current mood. He crossed the kitchen, scratching his belly and his hair at the same time. He grabbed a mug of black coffee and yawned, then took his first good look around. He saw me, forty-five minutes too early, the fresh coffee, and the three boxes of donuts. Then he focused his attention back on me.

"Sautel, you really are as stupid as you look," he growled. "You *know* I'm on a diet, and you're bringing all this sugar in here?"

He looked inside the closest box and grabbed a chocolate creme–filled donut. "Son of a . . . ," he muttered, leaving the kitchen and heading for the apparatus bay. "Guys like you are why I'm fat."

I turned away to hide my grin. A firehouse at shift-change might not be the place to find gratitude, but at least it was full of a certain kind of family.

—◇—

"Yo, *Seed*, I said what up?"

I must have pulled a surprised face. Not because of the nickname—Demon Seed had caught on right away, and I responded to it as often as my real name now—but because I'd been tuned *way* out. I'd been sitting alone at the far side of the dinner table, chair tipped back against the wall and hands locked behind my head. The electric clock had taken my attention for the last twenty minutes or so. I'd been pondering how it had stayed in that same spot for over fifty years and what it must have witnessed: older firefighters passing on wisdom to younger ones, the countless tall tales that had been traded around the dinner table, the counseling and consoling, the insults, and even a few fistfights.

Truth was, imagining stories about a clock was my way of *not* thinking about the family in apartment #312. It was only halfway working, but that was better than nothing.

Between the time I'd brought donuts and now, at 8:00 p.m., I'd been on six calls. Four medicals, one shooting, and one car wreck. Multiply that by every day on duty during my career, and I'd seen almost everything. You had to have pretty thick skin to do the job, but for some reason, more and more calls were getting stuck in my head.

"I see how it is . . . you're just gonna ignore me, right, Seed?"

I pulled my eyes away from the clock. "Not ignoring you, Rog," I replied, "just thinking."

Rog could tell something was up. We were family, not coworkers. And serving the Oakland community meant our family's health and safety had to be priority one.

"You get rejected by some girl," he guessed, "and now you can't stop thinking about her?"

I knew Rog was just starting things off. Even if that *was* what I'd been thinking about, he probably wouldn't have asked. Rog was a solid family guy, and religious too, so the stories of whatever craziness the younger guys were getting into held less interest for him. Didn't mean he'd walk away from any of our conversations, but everyone could tell he wasn't exactly impressed. If he was pushing me this hard for a conversation, it meant he suspected something was going wrong inside me.

That was bad news for a guy like me, who avoided eye contact most of the time and sharing his feelings all of the time. But I knew I could trust Rog, and I didn't have much of a choice anyway because he wasn't going to leave me alone. I leaned forward and let my chair fall back on all four legs, switching my arms into what I hoped was a bro-let's-keep-this-short pose.

"Jason, what's *actually* bothering you?" he asked.

I laughed.

He didn't.

"I asked what's bothering you, man."

Normally I'd hide behind humor or change the subject, but that wasn't going to fly now. Instead, I sighed and started talking. "You've been here, what, eighteen years? That's a lot of murders, fatality fires, suicides, and everything else that's broken, right?"

He nodded.

"In all that time, have certain calls stuck with you for some reason?"

"*Hell* yeah, kid, and some more than others."

He was smart enough to let his curse hang in the air a minute. Rog *never* cursed, so I understood he'd used that word on purpose to let me know how serious his answer was. In this case, the word was almost literal, though. Both of us had put on our boots and walked through hell as firefighters. He'd just been on the journey a lot longer than I had.

I looked back at the clock. Conversations like this needed time to simmer. I was willing to wait, because I knew he was coming at me brother to brother. He outranked me and had seniority, but he wasn't trying to talk down to me. He lived like we were on the same level. And what I was sensing from him was love. No other word for it. I could tell that he was standing in front of me because he loved me.

So as he slowly began talking, I listened, even though I couldn't really process everything he was saying. He told me a story about a thorn in his life and how he couldn't get it out. He said he chose not to let the pain of that thorn drag him down but instead used that pain to drive him to help others. Then he spoke about his faith and the different lessons he'd learned as a Christian. He talked about walking the walk and not just using the right words.

Everything he was saying made sense . . . and yet nothing he was saying made sense.

I could tell he believed every word with all his heart. And I knew he would literally die for me, or with me, which gave the conversation serious weight. But his words just weren't penetrating. Part of me wanted them to, but a darker part of me was already feasting on the false hope I figured he was feeding me.

"I love you, bro," he said. Seemed like the end of what he wanted to share.

"Thanks, Rog. You too," I said, and meant it. And he *knew* I meant it.

Then he stood there and considered me for a long moment. I could guess what was coming. He was about to ask me what I thought about his advice. We were about to enter stage two.

Except I was wrong. Without another word, he turned and left.

Huh. I tipped back my chair and considered the clock on the wall again. This time my mind wasn't wandering through five decades of firefighting history. Instead, I thought about how Rog processed his pain. The reek of our line of work attached itself to his soul just like it did to mine. If he was still getting blasted by negativity after twenty years, was that what I had to look forward to?

Rog had a tool kit that worked for him. But that was because he had faith. I figured he was like the electric clock, and his faith was the power cord. He could keep on ticking, decade after decade, because of it.

I figured I was unplugged. Or worse, flat-out broken.

—◇—

Sleeping at the firehouse was easy.

Any non-firefighter would have been up all night long. We had no air-conditioning and almost no ventilation. It was always noisy because of some combination of street-racing cars, loud arguments and fights, and emergency sirens. The apparatus bay on the other side of the wall housed a hot engine that rarely had a chance to cool down. And on top of that, there was the dispatch speaker. That thing didn't have a volume dial for a reason. It was *supposed* to wake you up. And on fire calls, we could hear the dispatcher *and* the people calling 911. Since the speaker could blare at any time, sleep ought to have been impossible.

Bizarrely, though—at least for firefighters—possibly waking to the sound of someone screaming, "My neighbor's house is burning!" didn't poison our sleep for the night. Every fire emergency was followed by the dispatcher asking for the location, and we knew every highway, street, and alleyway of the city. So if a call was near enough to respond, all we needed to do was gear up and sprint to the engine. But if the call was on the other side of town, then literally the best thing we could do was roll over and go back to sleep.

Somewhere around 3:00 a.m. I sprung awake.

It was the same nightmare. I'd been trapped in the janitor's closet again, unable to escape from the darkness and fear. I felt blinded by dread.

I leaped out of bed and crouched on the floor. The cement was cool against my bare feet. My bare chest and back were dripping with sweat. Slowly I stood, legs shaking. One hand ran fingers through my damp hair and the other adjusted my boxer shorts. My heart was beating loud enough to wake the dead.

I knew Jimmy, Rog, and Cappy were all asleep, so I stumbled to the bathroom and closed the door. Resting my hands on the sink, I forced myself to look up. The streetlights outside drew shadows below my eyes.

"Sautel, you're a big, tough fireman," I growled at the mirror.

In response I shivered. My whole body was wet. *Cold* wet.

Pull it together, Sautel.

I was a highly trained paramedic. I could lift and carry a two-hundred-pound victim through the fire to safety. So why did I feel like a little boy, whimpering for someone to comfort me and tell me everything was going to be okay? How was I supposed to help others when I couldn't even help myself?

As I stared into the mirror, the rest of the bathroom seemed to darken. The only thing I could see was a face staring back in terror. Something, someone, was trying to get me to connect the dots.

I twisted on the cold water, filled my hands, and splashed my face. Once, twice, three times. I looked up again. The terror had faded, but the gaze of a small child was still there.

Still looking for a way out, but still expecting the worst.

CHAPTER 7

JAWS OF LIFE

IT WAS 11:00 A.M., and I was stuck in line at the grocery store.

Three hours into my shift, Cappy had given me the green light to do a quick personal trip. My stuff was on the belt waiting to be booped. Scanning the racks, I learned that Brad Pitt may have fathered a secret love child with Oprah and that I could get three packs of watermelon gum for a buck.

It was a typical shopping trip: a quart of milk, a box of Raisin Bran, two apples, lunch meat, a loaf of bread, and some ice cream for the guys. Everything would fit into a single bag, and then I'd cram that bag into the firehouse fridge until I took it home the next morning. I didn't need much because I tended to eat out a lot at home. It was easier to keep my mind busy when I was ordering sushi in a busy café or watching sports in a crowded bar. Wolfing down a baloney sandwich at the kitchen table in a way-too-quiet house held no appeal for me, but a guy couldn't eat out *every* meal.

I eyed the blue-haired lady in front of me. She was an extreme couponer who kept discovering one more in her purse. The woman in line behind me banged a package of frozen chicken onto the belt just a bit harder than she needed to. I knew that move, because I used it myself on occasion. It was like, "Oops, I didn't mean to do that, but now that you're looking my way . . ."

I was wearing my uniform: a dark-blue button-up shirt, badge, blue wool pants, and polished duty boots. If I'd been in board shorts, a T-shirt, and sandals, I knew the chicken never would've been banged down. I turned to see a gorgeous brunette dressed in high heels, stockings, a tight skirt, and an expensive blouse. We stayed professional when we were on duty, but it would have been *unprofessional* to ignore a fellow Oakland citizen.

"So . . . ," she opened, "what do you do for a living?"

Unless I was impersonating a fireman or on my way to a morning bachelorette party, I had to be a fireman. But she knew that. She just didn't want to skip right to the "So, you're a fireman . . ." line. Fine by me. I had a recycled answer for these situations.

"I'm just a toolbox for human tragedy."

She frowned. "A toolbox for tragedy?"

"It means the only thing I'm good at is helping people. Car crashes, house fires, the occasional cat in a tree. It's what we do at the OFD, Station 11."

"You guys *really* rescue cats out of trees? I thought that was a joke!"

"It's not as hot or glamorous as a three-alarm fire, but yeah, we do it all."

Her voice sounded like a college girl at a party when she responded, "I think pulling cats out of trees is *super* hot."

The cashier was now booping my stuff, and she contributed a sarcastic laugh and an eye roll. I tended to agree with her assessment of the conversation, so I decided to turn the topic away from myself. "What kinda work you do?" I asked.

"Angela Mendoza, trial lawyer," she pronounced, opening her fancy purse. "Here's my business card."

I noted her office was in the financial district in San Francisco. That meant she lived in Oakland Hills with all the other Richie Rich types and commuted. Time to scoot. I tucked her card into my pocket, then handed the cashier a twenty-dollar bill and told her to put the change in the March of Dimes container.

My new high-dollar lawyer friend could see I was leaving sooner than she'd hoped. "You better call me, or I'll have to call 911 and personally request Fireman Sautel to come and get my cat outta my tree!"

I laughed, winked—why not?—and turned to leave. *Wait a sec, how did she know my name?* I turned back and asked.

"It's on your name tag." She smiled, tapping my chest. For a smart guy I could sure be dumb sometimes.

When I started up my truck, I looked in the rearview mirror and saw Angela climb into a red BMW. The black hole inside me felt like it was daring me to follow up with her. Daring me to see how fast I could screw things up or, more likely, to see how fast I would realize I wasn't chasing anything good in the first place. I tossed the business card onto the seat next to me and headed back to the station.

Later that day, as we were putting a little extra shine on the fire engine with a fresh coat of wax, dispatch alerted us to a call: "Four-vehicle accident. Victims trapped. Northbound 980 at the 24 interchange. Units due . . ."

That was all we needed to spring into action, but this call was a bit ambiguous. Four-vehicle accident with victims trapped could mean quite a few things. It could be a fender bender, except with one of the cars suffering a heavy enough impact to warp the door and trap the driver. In that case we'd just peel open the car like a giant can of tuna and then direct traffic until the flatbed tow truck showed up. But it could also mean something gnarly had gone down.

My turnout coat and helmet were still next to the engine, and shrugging on the coat gave me a wonderful whiff of stale sweat and smoke. The Folgers commercial ran through my head. "The best part of wakin' up . . ."

Ten minutes later we were close enough that I could see a jack-knifed big rig. That was never *good* exactly, but sometimes it wasn't so bad. If an eighteen-wheeler decides to fold in two on the highway or a frontage road around 3:00 a.m., the surrounding lanes tend to be deserted. Jackknife a truck in those conditions—due to a rainstorm, say, or a deer bounding in front of the rig—and chances are the driver eventually climbs down from the cab, takes a deep breath, calls a heavy-duty tow truck, and sits down to wait.

Jackknifing on a busy freeway during the day meant something very different. More than likely the truck had just come from the Port of Oakland, since it was carrying one of those shipping containers. Oakland was one of the top ten busiest ports in the country, and it seemed like there was a 24/7 army of trucks unloading and reloading containers. The GVW (gross vehicle weight) on those loaded trucks was around forty tons, which was like stacking up ten minivans on top of each other.

As we slowed our approach, Cappy assessed the situation. Was the trailer upright or was it leaning? Had the stuff inside shifted? Was it in danger of tipping? If so, what was holding it up? He must not have seen anything out of the ordinary that would endanger us, so he told us to "Go get 'em" as we braked to a stop.

Our crew operated like a well-oiled machine. Cappy knew I would quickly approach each car and check for victims. My first job was to assess how badly people were hurt so Cappy could either radio for more help or cancel any extra help that was already en route. Rog would be putting out cones and then making sure me and Jimmy had the tools we needed. The cab on the eighteen-wheeler was still attached to the trailer and resting on all ten wheels. That almost certainly meant the driver would've been able to exit the cab. In front of the cab I saw two other cars that were almost totaled, but each had at least one door open, so those folks had probably gotten free as well—whether under their own power or pulled out by a passerby. Other arriving responders would figure out where they were and assess them.

My heart dropped when I spotted the fourth vehicle. It was underneath the trailer and wedged right up against the rear axle. The car looked more like a piece of road debris than an actual automobile. Broken glass covered the ground, and the wreck sat atop a syrupy puddle of oil and gasoline. I could see the rear bumper, license plate, and taillights protruding from the wreckage, and after that the rest of the vehicle disappeared into a dark cave of tangled metal.

Cappy approached to see what we needed.

"We haven't been under here yet," I told him, gesturing at the mangled car.

He did a quick 360 and came to the same conclusion I'd reached: going under was the only option we had to access what was pretty much a passenger-car pancake.

Our tool kit for operations like this included a few essentials. No matter the particulars of the crash, we always brought an ax and a pry bar. The ax could be used to hit the pry bar into a doorjamb so we could pry the door open with nothing more than brute strength. On something like this, though, we'd need mechanical assistance, which came in the form of a ladder truck from another company that rolled up on scene. Unlike our engine, they'd have cutters and spreaders—operated hydraulically by a power unit—that most people knew as "the jaws of life."

"Cappy," I said. "I'm going under to see if anyone's alive."

We both knew that someone surviving that kind of crash was next to impossible. But we couldn't assume anything, because assumptions quickly lead to death in our line of work.

I calculated the probability of life and death. There was a tiny chance that someone could have survived, which meant I needed to get moving. On the other hand, the chance was so small that I was probably dealing with a recovery, which meant I could take my time. On rescues, when someone's survival is on the line, *any* delay can mean the difference between life and death. Whether the need for speed takes the form of shedding your bulky safety gear and entering a tight space without protection or simply charging into an inferno without a hose line to make a rescue attempt, it always means increased risk for the firefighters. With recoveries, though, safety is of the essence. When the victims are already dead, they are now bodies that need to be recovered, so we slow it down. No need to add to the body count.

Still, I couldn't guarantee this was a recovery until I got under the trailer to make sure. Most people would look at a scene like this and say there was no way a person could survive such a violent force that had devoured this car and turned it into a flattened piece of metal. But we'd seen people survive crazier conditions. Not often, but often enough.

Helmet? Yeah, I wanted to wear my lid. Not that it could save me from everything, but it was still a lot better than even my admittedly thick skull. I crouched and squinted under the trailer. No way I'd fit with my helmet on.

Fine. I took my helmet off and handed it to Jimmy. "This shouldn't take long," I told him, and then wriggled forward on my hands and knees.

It was a picture-perfect day in Oakland, with bright sunshine and a sea breeze, but beneath the wreck it was dark. I had a flashlight attached to my turnout coat with a carabiner, but it wasn't shining more than a few inches in front of me because of the tight space I was in. I could feel the rough pavement scratching my knees as I crawled beneath the underbelly of the big rig. It was only a few feet, but with the broken glass, the smell of fresh gasoline, and tons of metal sitting inches above my head, it felt like I had been tunneling for a mile. Since there was no room for anyone to come in beside me, Jimmy followed behind.

I reached out and touched the car with my fingertips. "Anyone in there?"

It felt like a ridiculous question, given the state of the vehicle, but it was a lot better than shouting, "Is anyone alive in there?" If someone was alive, the first question would give them a measure of power. The second would likely make them panic.

"I'm alive!" a man's voice answered.

I flinched and bashed the back of my head on whatever piece of metal was above me. I tried to play it cool, like I'd been expecting an answer. Like, *of course* someone was alive, and *of course* I'd get him out.

"Hey!" I called. "How are you?"

"Not good. I can't move. I'm hurting bad."

I could tell from his clipped sentences that he was struggling to even get the words out. Probably struggling to breathe. That would explain the fear that covered his voice like a hand over a flashlight.

"How many are with you?" I asked.

"Two of us, but—"

I waited.

"Two—"

I waited. I inched forward a bit more and finally reached the passenger door. There was just enough room for me to kneel.

"Hey," I said to the man, reaching for my flashlight.

"Two of us," he tried again, "but she's dead."

I played the beam of my flashlight across the door, the empty window frame, the misshaped interior of the car, and the underbelly of the trailer. I looked at everything real casual-like, but really, I was confirming the man's diagnosis. Half a second of light on the woman's crumpled body confirmed what he told me.

"I'm gonna talk to my guys now," I told the man, "and then we'll get to work."

Jimmy backed out. I pivoted on one knee and leaned my head down so I could yell back toward the sunlight. "Cappy! One injured and entangled, one deceased."

Cappy, crouching, looked like an almost-upside-down silhouette against the almost-white sky. He acknowledged, then his almost-upside-down silhouette leaned toward me and sniffed. "You crawl through gasoline?"

I definitely had. It had already soaked through the knees of my pants, but there was no way I was getting pulled back now for safety reasons. "Nope!" I lied. "I can smell it but didn't crawl through it."

Jimmy was already on the same page. He came back in behind me with a hose line and opened it just enough to thin out the leaking gasoline without flooding the scene or taking my head off. He set it down and told me, "The truck guys are setting up the jaws and will feed them into us. Seeing as it's so tight, we can switch off when you get tired. But until then, just call me your pack mule."

He scurried back toward the light, and I heard the power unit roar to life. It would send an ungodly amount of power into the cutting tools through two long cables filled with hydraulic fluid. But power wasn't the issue. Space was. I turned back toward the car. A few seconds later I heard the sounds of Jimmy returning to our metal tunnel with the spreader tool. He patted my calf to let me know and then pushed the spreader through my legs and up against the door of the car. I had never used them alone. Usually we surrounded the mangled car and attacked it as a team, but this wreck didn't want to cooperate.

Spreaders looked basically like scissors, except they weighed eighty pounds and their force was directed outward. So . . . nothing like normal scissors. Point is, I could ram them into a crack or gap of any size and then use the hydraulic power to widen the gap. I wrestled the spreader into position and got the passenger door to pop free almost instantly, but I still had to do something with it. Doing my best contortionist impression, I tried to act like Spider-Man, but my 220-pound frame and the tiny space made me look more like Al Bundy. I managed to get the door flat under my feet just far enough behind me for Jimmy to pull it.

"Pull!" I yelled.

"Bro, take your weight off of it, you fat ass!" he grunted, struggling to pull it.

I grabbed the top of the car and lifted myself up just enough for him to tug it free. With the door out of the way, I had access to a terrifying and terrifyingly tiny space. Three adults wouldn't have fit comfortably in the front of that car under normal circumstances—and these circumstances were an awful long way from normal.

Out of habit I checked the woman, feeling her neck for a pulse. Deceased. So right now I needed to concentrate on the driver.

I aimed my flashlight beam across the windshield, dashboard, and console. What I saw was not encouraging. The entire front end of the car had been pushed toward the occupants and then folded downward when the truck's weight rode up on it. It appeared as if the occupants had no legs. That meant I wouldn't be able to extract the deceased passenger's body and pass it back to Jimmy. Instead, I'd have to switch to the cutting tool, then lay across the woman's lap to reach the driver. But with the dashboard pushed so far in, the only way to lay across the woman was to lean her seat back.

I knew this model had manual seats, so I reached for the recline lever and pulled it. Her seat dropped, but only a few inches. The back seat and roof were too compressed to allow it to recline any farther.

It's not your emergency, Sautel. Do what you need to do.

I'd have to treat her as part of the car or the ground. Another obstacle to overcome. I passed the spreader back to Jimmy and told him to push the cutter up. I set my flashlight on the remains of the dashboard so I'd have some light without needing to hold it. My number one priority was getting this man out, but I had to keep him talking. A calm voice in the midst of chaos gives hope, and hope was literally all this guy had to hang on to.

"All right, sir, the hard part's over. Let's get you outta here!"

It was a lie. The hardest part had just started. But whatever. I reached forward with my left hand and grabbed the headrest of the man's seat, while with my right I gripped the cutter. I scrabbled behind me with my boots until I found something solid. Then I pushed and pulled and wriggled my way across the passenger's body. Her head flopped forward until it rested warm in the crook of my neck.

"What's your name?" I asked calmly.

A pause. Then, "Bill."

"Where were you headed, Bill?"

Another pause. "Work."

Time for me to work. I was in my office, but my office was this guy's nightmare, and both of us were running out of time. The steering wheel had to go first. The impact had shoved it basically inside his chest, and I could tell his whole torso was under immense pressure. I muscled the cutter into place.

"What. Are. You. Doing?" he managed.

"Gonna cut that wheel away," I said, "so we can get you breathing better."

I raised the cutter, mostly with one hand, and managed to get it behind the steering wheel and around the column. The lactic acid in my forearms was becoming an issue, as my right arm was starting to shake.

I blinked to clear away the sweat from my eyes, but more sweat took its place. The cutter made quick work of the steering column. I set down the cutter and grabbed the steering wheel, lifting it away from the man's chest. With the pressure relieved it was easier for him to breathe, but not by much, given the broken ribs he'd obviously suffered. I passed the steering wheel behind me toward Jimmy until I felt him take it. The woman's head shifted on my neck and I felt its warmth again. I blinked, and the sweat-sting got even worse.

The parking brake had to go next. It would interfere if I tried to pull the man toward me. Then the seat belt for sure, followed maybe by the dashboard. I hefted the cutter again.

"Gonna snip this off," I told the man. "That'll make it easier to pull you out."

His only response was a series of quick breaths and a sort of shuddering whisper.

I activated the cutter. *Snuh-tick!* Brake lever cut. I passed it back and then cut the seat belt with my trusty pocketknife. I risked a look at the man's face. His cheeks were wet and his eyes were fluttering.

"Who was your passenger?" I kept my voice level.

"Lady," he answered. "Took her. To work. Car pool."

I looked back to the cabin. I thought maybe if I switched to the spreader I could push the crumpled dashboard away from the man's legs. But what would I brace the spreader on? What if there was no room for the dashboard to move into? *Or I could try cutting the—*

"She was. Choking," the man said, gasping for air himself. "Before. You guys. Showed up."

I raised the cutter and spread its blades to maximum width.

"She cried. For help. I couldn't. I didn't know. I—"

I struggled to wedge the blades around part of the dashboard.

"I think. She died. Right when. I heard. Your sirens."

Crump. The cutter sliced through their target, but there was nothing I could remove. I'd need to make another cut, and another, and start removing wedges. My eyes and forearms were a wreck. I lifted the cutter, spread the blades, and picked a new target.

"When I heard. Sirens. I got. Some hope."

Crump. Crump. I set down the cutter and tried to find a handhold on a piece of dashboard so I could tug it free and pass it back.

"Otherwise. Woulda been. Just me. In here."

He was preaching to the choir. Being trapped inside dark spaces was kind of my thing.

There. I pulled a section of dashboard free and wrestled it back. I felt Jimmy take its weight. What next? I grabbed my flashlight and aimed it toward the man's legs and almost dropped it. I didn't drop it because I was a stone-cold lifesaver—but I almost did.

His lower legs were just . . . rolled up. Rolled up inside some part of the dashboard or firewall. My heart dropped. Under ideal conditions, unrolling the dashboard off a trapped person's legs takes a team, including someone standing on the hood of the car. I was running out of options, but I refused to quit.

"Am I. Gonna die?"

"Not on my watch!" I snapped back. "We're getting out of here together, my friend."

I almost said something else, but the lump in my throat forced me to clamp my jaw shut. That was twice in one week. *Stone-cold lifesaver my ass.*

On the streets of Oakland, I'd witnessed extraordinary feats. I'd once seen a heartbeat appear on our heart monitor as we were doing CPR on a kid who had zero chance of survival—and the doctors had zero explanation. So we refused to give up. *Cromp. Cromp.* Another chunk free. But his legs were still just as trapped.

Hard-core emergencies were basically the Olympics of survival. You had one shot. This man was at the starting line of the 100-meter finals or on the edge of the 10-meter platform. His entire *being* was focused on performing a single, achingly simple, probably impossible physical task: breathing.

In, then out. In. Out. In. Out. In. Out.

In.

Out.

His body started to vibrate like a lake in a windstorm. I set down my cutter. There was no tool for what was about to happen. I placed both hands under his jaw and carefully manipulated his head to open his airway. It wouldn't make an ounce of difference to his survival. All I hoped was that a few more real breaths would ease his pain. And maybe that he would feel the skin of my fingers and palms on the skin of his jaw, his cheek, his neck. That in his last moments he would feel a human touch.

I found the magic angle to open his airway all the way. His shuddering stopped like someone had flicked a switch. His chest rose and fell in silence.

Tears ran down his right cheek in a single streak. Every time he gasped, another drop flowed down the wet mark and disappeared.

In.

Out.

In.

Out.

Then . . . nothing. No movement. No last words. Just nothing. There was no glory. Just the last exhale of a desperate body clawing for every millisecond of life.

I am so sorry. I should have been here sooner. I should have pulled you out faster. I'm so, so, so, so sorry. I let my head fall. Closed my eyes tight. *Sautel, you failed again!*

Tap, tap, went Jimmy's hand on my right boot. I was the tip of the spear on this recovery-then-rescue-then-recovery, and he wanted to know why I'd stopped working.

I turned my head and yelled, "Back out!"

Everything in reverse. I extracted the cutting tool from the cabin of the wreck. I crawled backward over the body of the woman in the passenger seat. I hit my knees on the ground, then shuffled by feel toward the light that I knew was behind me. The sunshine blinded me as I finally unfolded upright. My arms felt like they weighed a hundred pounds. I set down the tool, collected my helmet, and put it on, then straightened fully.

"Both dead," I said.

My hands rose toward my face. Blood, sweat, and grime traced them. I shoved my hands into my pockets to stop the shaking.

None of the guys said a word. They knew what I knew.

I exhaled long and slow. Twenty steps to the engine, two steps to climb into my seat, and then I finally let my head fall into my hands. Let my shoulders crumple. The grime and sweat stung my already stinging eyes, and I didn't give a damn.

CHAPTER 8
DRESS CODE

MY KITCHEN WAS DARK. Lights were off, blinds were closed, and only a bit of twilight snuck in. But I could still see the mess I'd made on the floor: an explosion of blue ceramic, cornflakes, an upside-down spoon, and a spreading pool of milk. I could see it so well, despite the darkness, because of where I was, curled up on the linoleum, right beside the remains of my meal, clutching my stomach in agony.

It was Saturday evening, and I hadn't eaten since Thursday night. It didn't look like that would be changing anytime soon. The instant the first bite of cereal hit my stomach, I'd doubled over in pain, dropping the bowl. A second wave of pain hit, worse than the first, and I'd flopped on the floor beside the shattered bowl. It was pure torture. I had no idea what had just happened, but I suspected it was more than just physical. That sounded like crazy talk, but I could feel yesterday's call inside me somewhere. Maybe it was making me literally sick.

Eventually the agonizing cramping faded, and I managed to drag my sorry butt off the ground and clean up the mess.

Sleep. If I couldn't eat, the least I could do was rest my body and, hopefully, shut out the world—and images of yesterday—for a few hours.

But there was a problem with that plan. I always slept in a noiseless environment at home. At the firehouse I could sleep through anything, but at home it was different. The slightest noise would set my nerves on edge and rev up my heart. So I had a habit of closing all the blinds and turning out all the lights in the house, ending with my bedroom. Then, when it was perfectly dark and quiet, I could maybe catch some Z's.

Not this time.

I went through my bedtime routine, but the moment I turned the last light off, something evil turned on.

It had been waiting just out of sight, behind the curtains and inside closets, under the couch and under my bed. And in the dark it came oozing out, filling my bedroom. I wasn't like a little kid worried about the boogeyman in the closet. Pitch darkness never bothered me. This was something new and all too real.

I could feel it on my skin as I lay in bed. It inserted itself into my mind as something far worse than mere darkness. I felt like I was trapped watching a scary movie with no way to turn it off. No way to free myself and turn on the lights. Something else was controlling my mind, and somehow I knew I'd be watching the same horror show all night long.

I shivered. Quickly I flicked my bedroom light back on, then continued through the rest of the house. I turned on the radio and turned up the volume. Anything was better than waiting in the silent darkness.

It looked like food and sleep were going to have to wait. But there was no way I was going to let the evil have its way with me without putting up a fight. I rubbed my eyes in exhaustion. My plan for the night became very simple: survive until the sun came up.

What followed was an hours-long slideshow of awfulness. Each memory like a punch in the gut. A body blow.

The time I made a big deal about it being my birthday and invited kids from my class to my dad's place for a sleepover. Except as soon as the kids saw my room—a mattress, dirty clothes on the floor, and nothing else—they wanted to call their moms and get picked up early. I tried to convince them to stay by feeding them. Baloney slices and white bread. Freezer-burned ice cream scooped into dirty bowls and eaten with spoons taken out of the sink. We saw a cockroach scrabble across the linoleum.

The time my fourth-grade teacher yelled at me in front of the class because my report about the state of Florida was a failure. I'd tried hard, but the library was on the other side of town, too far to walk after walking home from school. As punishment, my teacher sent me to the first-grade classroom for a week, where I hunched, miserable, in a desk built for someone a foot shorter.

The time, when I was only eleven, that I decided to start hanging out with older kids who smoked weed and drank alcohol. Eleven seemed old enough. Old enough to break into houses with them too, and steal liquor or tear up a drained pool with our skateboards.

The time my dad pulled over at a roadside swap meet and told me I could choose a framed picture of a fancy car for my birthday. Except the one I chose, a white Ferrari, cost two dollars more than the other pictures. "Payday is still a week out and bills are due," he said. "Go ask the man where the ten-dollar ones are." I just got back in the truck feeling like a kid who wasn't worth two dollars.

The time after time after time when I'd trudge home the two miles from school, desperate for anything to happen that didn't hurt, only to be hurt the second I stepped through the door. Berated for things beyond my control, which made me ignore him, even if he was right. Sometimes it felt like my only crime was being me.

Punch after punch after punch. I felt each one as I relived the memories. It was torture—but as long as the lights were on, I figured I could survive. I figured I could make it until morning.

But then what?

—◇—

Sometime toward morning I heard a voice in my head.

Maybe you should go to church, Sautel.

Where in the world had *that* thought come from? And why the hell would going to church for the first time be a good plan after two-plus days of no food, no sleep, and a night of agony?

But then I started to consider the idea for real. Not church in general, but the specific one a few blocks away from my house. Any Sunday morning I was home, usually having coffee on my porch, I'd see a bunch of happy people walking past. They didn't quite match what Dad had always told me about church people when I was a kid. Like how they were a bunch of fakers and always in his way when he was trying to get to the store on Sundays. He figured they were all a bunch of hypocrites.

But these church people were always smiling. I pictured them smiling at me in the morning, and a tiny feeling of hope started to shine in my dark mind. Maybe their smiles were plastered on and fake like my dad had believed. Maybe they were as hypocritical as he'd warned. But as the night wore on, I couldn't bring myself to care about hypocrisy. To me, insincere smiles were better than no smiles at all.

Finally the sun rose. I felt like I'd fought a six-alarm fire by myself. My stomach was still cramping periodically, and my eyes felt like someone had rubbed sandpaper across them. But I'd survived the night, and now it was time to try out that church.

I'd walked by the church a million times, usually on my way to one of my favorite bars, so I was familiar with the sign outside:

8 AM   Traditional Sunday Service

10 AM   Contemporary Service

I had no idea what any of that meant. All I knew was that there were two options, and waiting an extra two hours to feel better didn't make any sense. So I made myself presentable with clean khaki shorts, a fresh T-shirt, and my newest pair of Vans. I splashed some water on my face and tried to blink away my exhaustion. I knew going to church for the first time wouldn't be a walk in the park. Getting hope or a smile or love or whatever it was I was trying for was going to be a lot tougher than going into the liquor store and coming out two minutes later with a six-pack.

In the past, Christians had scared me. They'd always been real clear about where things stood: they were going to heaven and I was going to hell. But at least these Christians smiled. I was desperate enough to cling to that.

I needed to time my arrival right. Get there too early and they might find out how horrible of a person I was and kick me out. Arrive too late and the doors might be locked, or everyone might stare at me while I found the last empty seat in the front row.

I closed the front door and started down the block. Was there a way I was supposed to walk to church? Maybe walking with a purpose would be good—but what if I looked like the pastor's pet? Or maybe a casual stroll was better, like I accidentally arrived right when the service was beginning—but what if I looked like I didn't care about being there? I settled on walking with a purpose, but casually. This church stuff was turning out to be harder than I'd thought.

As I walked up to the building, I started to feel a bit twitchy. All the guys had slacks on, and some were even wearing coats and ties. The ladies wore dresses and heels. Even the kids had tucked-in shirts and gelled-down hair. My self-consciousness started to flare. It felt like I was back in middle school.

Being an outcast had always been the norm for me. Like in eighth grade, when I needed a PE uniform and took the cost breakdown to my dad. He ignored it, then yelled at me when I reminded him. At school, my PE coach made an example of me every day that year, calling me up to the front to start every class. "Look at you in your raggedy clothes, Sautel. Even a *PE* uniform would be better than the trash you dress in! You think you're too good to follow the rules? You think you're better than the other kids here? You're not. You're worse!"

Now here I was, once again, an outcast. That seemed to be the one role in life I could always count on. I gave myself a mental slap. *Come on, Sautel! Quit judging these people. They're probably nice, and you're an Oakland firefighter who wins awards working with your brothers at the firehouse to save lives. Drop your stupid insecurities and move on!*

The closer I got to church, the thicker the crowd got. Everyone held a Bible, and everyone smiled. Walking casually but purposefully, I plastered a smile on my tired face and turned toward the front door. I saw the family walking in front of me enter the church. I was almost there.

Suddenly I pulled up short. Two men were standing at the front door, one on either side, and their body language was absolutely shouting, "Halt!"

I was well versed on how to handle situations where I was an unwelcome guest. But my brain was probably exaggerating the situation after what I'd suffered through the night before. This was a church, right? It wasn't like I would need to fight my way inside. I'd just smile like everyone else—well, everyone else besides these two gatekeepers—and head inside.

"How's it going?" I asked in my friendliest voice, moving toward the door. Then I added a little joke, "I didn't realize this church had bouncers!"

My wisecrack did *not* improve their body language. One crossed his arms and puffed up his chest. The second took half a step toward me. "You can't come in *here*," the man said slowly, "dressed like *that*." His voice dripped with mockery.

I was stunned. There I was, beat down, tired, hurting, hungry, and in need of a piece of whatever happiness seemed to be inside that place, and he wasn't going to let me in? *And* he was going to mock me for my appearance?

"Why?" That single word was all I could manage.

The man glared at me and crossed his arms. "You have to go."

"This is why I hate you stupid church people," I said, then spun around and started to walk away. Tears welled up in my eyes. I could feel the two guys following me, so I turned around, yelling, "What's your problem?" It was one of the most honest questions I'd ever asked. I truly didn't understand what was happening.

"This church is private property. Leave. Now!"

I made my way back up the street, scraping the tears off my cheeks. I promised myself I'd never set foot in a church again.

But I knew that wasn't completely true. If I was on duty, or even if I was off duty, I'd lay my life on the line to save anyone in that church, including the two guys who had just made me feel like I was nothing. That was my job: to treat, not judge. I could have flashed my badge to prove I was one of the good guys, but I chose to let them believe what they wanted about me. All because . . . what? Because I didn't look like I *belonged* in their church?

I was all too familiar with how bad it hurts to be judged and kicked aside. This was just one more lesson. But this time it hurt worse than usual because the ones who were mistreating me were the ones I'd actually tried to take a chance on. All I wanted was to feel the same love and acceptance everyone else walking into that church seemed to have. I wanted to smile a real smile, to hug and be hugged back. I wanted someone to tell me there was a way to be okay. I wanted someone to help me fight whatever the darkness was inside me.

There was no way I was going back home after what I'd just

suffered through the night before. I walked around my neighborhood at random, seething at the rejection. It felt just like Christmas at my grandparents' when I was sixteen. My dad had been there with his girlfriend and her kid.

"Merry Christmas," he told her kid, producing a wrapped present. "This is for you."

As a boy I'd always felt guilty when I opened a gift because he would always remind me of how much it cost. So when he gave that present to his girlfriend's kid, I lost it. I was done. How many birthdays had he taken me out for a meal only to complain about what it was costing him while I tried to choke down the food? How many Christmases had I slogged through feeling like an afterthought, less important than the faded tinsel on our crooked, plastic Christmas tree? I snapped. We got in each other's faces, but before anyone needed an ambulance, I stalked out the door, climbed into my Ford Fairlane, and fired it up. I drove back to Dad's place, grabbed the emergency cash he always kept in the top drawer of his dresser, and got back in the car. Then it was eight hours north, mostly on Interstate 5, toward my mom's place. I thought about going head-to-head with a big rig, but something inside told me to keep pushing.

Just like something inside me now couldn't stop crying. The memory brought me to a halt with a shudder. The rejection I'd just experienced at the church felt the same—except this time I no longer had any urge to keep pushing.

What in the . . . ?

I put a hand on my chest and felt around. Blinked and twitched like I was insane, then dropped my hand as my shoulders slumped.

Because the thing that had been tormenting me, that had been living inside me, that had been taunting me since I was a child as it clawed away every scrap of happiness . . . was gone.

And that was the worst news possible.

I understood it wasn't gone because it had been defeated. It was gone because it had defeated *me*. The darkness had won. Now it could move on to its next victim. I was already a goner.

At least there's an end in sight.

The thought was strangely welcome. I had finally been beaten into submission by whatever it was that was stealing my life. Now the fight was over.

Forget this world and everyone in it.

I tried that thought on for size, and it fit me perfectly.

So this is what hopelessness feels like. Sautel, you thought you had a right to hope? What a joke. I'd been clinging to the last thread at the end of my rope, and now I could just . . . let go.

I started walking again. On the outside I looked like a tough guy, but I was really a lost kid who'd just realized calling for help was pointless. An eerie sense of calm washed over me. Numbness.

At least now I could go back to sleeping with the lights off. There was no point in hiding from the inevitable.

CHAPTER 9
READY

SURFING THE SONOMA COAST was no joke, especially for a novice like me.

I'd learned to surf back in high school, before I dropped out. Some buddies and I would ditch class and drive to San Clemente or San Onofre for the day.

As a firefighter in Oakland, I'd started to surf again. Partly for the occasional glimpse of peace and tranquility, but more for the adrenaline shot of dealing with the gnarly conditions on California's central coast. Between the water temp—which was take-your-breath-away cold, even with a wetsuit on—the swirling currents, and waves that could get scary-big, surfing was something I could count on to drown out everything else in my life.

Oh, and the sharks. They kept a lot of other people out of the water and me on my toes. Even getting to my favorite break could be dangerous. The drive along the famous and famously twisty Pacific Coast Highway featured sheer drops, sudden fog banks, and California drivers.

I'd arrived home from the firehouse around nine in the morning and had planned to go out for a session at Salmon Creek. Instead, I'd spent the next couple of hours just staring into the bathroom mirror trying to figure out who or what was staring back. I wondered if I could see in my own eyes what I'd seen in the eyes of that Bay Bridge jumper.

Turned out I was done. Finished.

What I saw in the mirror helped me be completely honest with myself. I wasn't a hero or even a helper. I was just a guy who ruined everything he touched. I wasn't the good guy I wanted to be, and I never would be.

Honestly, staring in the mirror had been time well spent. The clarity was calming. At last I was ready to grab my board and hit the water. I walked through the kitchen and into the garage to gather my surf gear. I kept my board—a stable but fast seven-foot, six-inch Channel Islands—in a cloth board bag on a padded rack I'd built into a wall of the garage. My wetsuit, booties, and hood hung beneath it. I tapped the button to open the garage and loaded my board and wetsuit into my truck.

Once my board and the rest of what I needed was stowed in the bed, I walked back inside. I took my cell phone out of my shorts pocket and set it on the kitchen table. I didn't want any distractions once I headed out. Then I went into the guest room and grabbed a piece of paper and pen from the desk before returning to the kitchen. I sat at the kitchen table and wondered how many hours I had spent in that spot, eating alone—too many times to count.

I rested one hand on the paper and held the pen with the other. With the tip of the pen hovering over the paper, I did an internal inventory. Calm. Relaxed. *Okay.* I nodded once and waited a minute or two. Yep, this was the right thing. Completely at peace.

The only thing I felt was concern for my family and friends. I knew my mom and dad and sister would miss me in their own ways, but I was feeling distant from them. My deeper worry was for my eleven-year-old niece, Bethany. Over the years I'd managed to fly back a few times to my sister's place in North Carolina to see her. Hanging with Bethany was one of the only bright spots in my life. I just hoped she'd be young enough to forget all about me. My biggest dread was that I'd hurt my OFD friends. They felt like my real family, really. I started writing to them, and the concern, the care, flowed onto the paper. The cruelest thing I could do was allow them to pretend I might be coming back. I couldn't give them any hope that they'd see me again. I was going to make this as painless as possible for everyone in my life, including the first responders. Especially them.

Every single one of us had flashbacks that haunted us. Seeing a body hanging or with half its head missing—that kind of thing embeds itself in your memory. It might stay dormant for a time, then come alive when you least expect it to. It might wake you up in the middle of the night or visit you during a holiday celebration. No way was I going to become a gruesome memory embedded in another first responder's psyche.

No. I needed everyone to know I was gone. Really gone. Not gone-on-a-surprise-vacation, but *gone* gone.

I reached the last line of my note. *I'm so sorry.*

One more internal inventory. Still good. Okay, time to go.

Jason.

I signed my name and set the pen down on the paper. Then I placed my cell phone on top of the paper as well. I stood and took one last look around the kitchen, then stepped through the door into the garage. Before climbing into my truck, I looked into its bed. At the front, just below the rear cab window, rested the two cinder blocks I'd placed there earlier, and a neatly coiled length of rope was secured underneath.

A forty-five-minute paddle, even with the extra weight of the cinder blocks, would get me a few miles into the Pacific. My plan was to tie one end of the rope to the cinder blocks and the other end around my ankles and then just roll off the board and into the water. My surfboard might eventually make its way back to shore, but the sea creatures would make sure no part of me did.

I climbed into my cab, shoved the keys into the ignition, and then, through the open cab window, heard my cell phone chirp from inside on the kitchen table. A flimsy door and less than ten feet separated me from it. I pressed on the key between my thumb and fingers. I could drown out the call if I started the engine, but I waited until the phone stopped.

I took a deep breath, then exhaled. *Okay, still peaceful.* My fingers tensed as I started to turn the key—and then my cell phone started chirping again.

Get it.

The voice in my head was insistent. I frowned.

Get it, get it, get it, get—

Fine. I climbed out, jogged back into the kitchen, grabbed my cell, and took the call.

"Hello?"

"Bro, I'm two minutes out, and I'm *craving* an organic spinach-and-feta omelet from that new place downtown. I'm taking you with me, so be ready!"

It was Chad, my San Francisco firefighter friend. We'd met at the gym and immediately hit it off. He was nothing like me. He was very particular about the food he put in his body, whereas a box of Cap'n Crunch seemed healthy enough to me. He loved going to the movies and partying, while I usually went only when I had to. He drove a fancy sports car, and I drove a truck. But our bond was untouchable and branded in fire.

"Chad, I'm headed out to surf."

"No prob, my dude," he said, "you can hit it with a belly full of your unhealthy waffles slathered in butter and syrup when we're done. See you in ninety!"

"Chad, I—"

Click.

On autopilot, my mind blank, I walked out to the driveway. Sixty seconds later Chad rolled up to the curb in his sports car and climbed out.

"Bro, I just got off work and drove straight here," he reported, running a hand through his hair. He looked like death warmed over. "Can we take your truck? We took a beating last night. Six runs after midnight."

I knew that feeling. After a night like that Chad was lucky to be speaking in mostly coherent sentences. I nodded. But then I could feel his eyes boring into me. Things got real quiet. Then, "Bro. Jason. You okay?"

"Why you asking?"

"Dunno, man, but you look . . . *different.*"

"Yeah, 'cause I'm going surfing."

"Nah, man, it's not that."

The only place I could manage to look was at the chest of his San Francisco Fire Department shirt. Their insignia was an eagle stretching out its wings, and underneath the eagle were two firemen. One of them was looking out to sea. Trying to keep people safe on the water. There were cliffs, waves, a tiny boat, and a horizon.

"You just got a look in your eyes, man."

I knew what he was seeing, even if I couldn't see it myself right then. I knew what was staring back at him, even if I wasn't.

First responders never stop responding. They size up every situation, every person they meet. I knew Chad had put two and two together and was hunting for a way to handle the situation he'd just walked into.

"Jason?"

I finally looked up.

"Come on, bro," he said, slapping my shoulder, "let's go grab you some waffles."

CHAPTER 10

MOTHER'S DAY

NO REST FOR THE weary. Not even the soul-weary.

In spite of how I'd intended to spend my day before Chad showed up, I enjoyed grabbing waffles with him.

Or at least I didn't hate it. After he drove off, I took out my surfboard and hung it on the rack, then stowed my wetsuit. I placed the cinder blocks and coil of rope back into the garage. Then I went inside and tossed my suicide note in the kitchen trash. After puttering around the house, I was able to catch a few hours of sleep without feeling fear. The empty blackness inside me was still there, but it hadn't gotten worse. I went back to work like nothing happened.

I guess because nothing *had* happened.

So it was back to the status quo for me. Back to being Jason "Demon Seed" Sautel, firefighter/paramedic, Oakland Fire Department, Station 11. Back to being alive, even though most days I felt like the walking dead. Thing is, status quo was still a long way from being okay.

Life filled up with the same old routine. Twenty-four hours on, forty-eight hours off. One day of trying to work hard enough to forget everything, then two days on pins and needles just waiting for the blackness to rear up again. The blackness felt like some kind of predator, ready to pounce on its prey. So I decided to isolate it. No going out with the guys, no looking for cute girls at the bar, no movies or exercise runs. That way if it did strike, at least I'd be the only one in its range.

What I really wanted was to put my past behind me forever.

Trying to forget the sadness of every shift was struggle enough—so when my brain piled on the memories of my childhood, it was overwhelming. Every call where I saw a kid whose eyes were filled with sadness took me back. Every fractured family reminded me of my own. Every second I spent crawling into darkness to fight fire forced part of my heart back into the janitor's closet, with the door held shut until I stopped crying for my mommy.

Most people had a baseline they could reset to, a foundation they could start to build on. But I figured anything I built would eventually collapse. I wanted relationships. Love. The same stuff everyone else around me wanted and seemed to have. I just knew I couldn't have what I wanted because the darkness would eat it.

It was a cool, foggy morning. I was cruising into work when I noticed a dozen motorcycles parked outside an abandoned warehouse just down the block from our firehouse. The bikes were big boys too— looked like Harleys with lots of customizations. The building was similar to the majority of warehouses on our side of town, made of old brick and mortar and heavy, burnable timber. Usually they were old steel and lumber mills, or heavy machine shops from a time when Oakland actually made stuff. Now they were just shells, used by sketchy businesses that were often fronts for something illegal.

Those buildings worried us. Driving home from calls, we'd talk tactics and guess at the interior layouts, just in case. With places like that, a raging fire was a matter of when, not if. When left abandoned, they were far from the worst danger in our city—except this one was now occupied.

I came into the firehouse and told Cappy what I'd seen. He said he noticed the same thing and asked, "Thinking we should go say hello to our new neighbors, Seed?"

I nodded. "Sure, but what are you gonna do, go knock on the front door?"

Cappy grinned. "Nah. Those guys may be inside now, but they like a little sunshine just like everyone else. Give it a few hours."

He was right. That afternoon, once the marine layer burned off, the four of us hopped on the fire engine and cruised by the warehouse to "inspect" it, seeing as how it had gone from vacant to occupied overnight. And sure enough, a dozen or so guys were outside. A few sitting on their bikes, a few fixing their bikes, and a few making out with leather-clad ladies. Most were smoking, and it seemed like all were drinking 40s of malt liquor.

Cappy eased to a stop in front of the warehouse and rolled down his window. Gave the group of guys an upward head nod and got a bunch of nods in return.

"Sooo . . . ," Cappy drawled, "you all opening a repair shop?"

Someone snickered. Someone else silenced the snickering guy with a look. Cappy waited. So did the alpha biker, who knew to let his underlings display his authority. About ten seconds later, every other biker was looking at one particular biker. The guy took a pull on his bottle for good measure, then spit.

"Nah . . . ," he drawled back to Cappy, "just hanging out at a new place."

Cappy nodded. I couldn't see his face, but I could tell by the thumbs-up he gave and received that they mutually understood each other. I'd been working with the guy a long time, and it was about the millionth time he was incredibly cool under pressure.

As we headed back to the firehouse, Cappy snorted. "Just what we need, *another* biker gang in the neighborhood. At least we'll keep getting our paychecks."

Oakland already had one biker gang, and it wasn't small potatoes. As far as those things went, it ran the show in Oakland and across most of the country. Drugs, prostitution, breaking and entering. No *bueno* for sure, but not usually on our plates. Oakland Police dealt with them, unless there happened to be a Molotov cocktail involved that set something on fire or they roughed someone up to prove a point.

Two gangs, though—that was bad. If we were real lucky, the leather holsters I'd seen on the bikes were just for looks and not for guns. But I had a feeling they weren't there just to socialize and rebuild carburetors.

That night me, Jimmy, and Rog were in our dorm. At 10:00 p.m., we always shut off the bright overhead lights and used the reading lamps next to our bunks. The bright lights above us never stayed off for long, though, since any time an alarm came in, the lights automatically kicked on just as the bell rang. Jimmy was already snoring, Rog was reading a paperback, and I was just lying there with my hands laced behind my head.

I heard Rog moving around and glanced over. He'd just picked up a boot from beside his bed and was lining up a throw toward Jimmy's bed when all hell broke loose outside. The distinct sound of high-caliber rifle fire erupted from what felt like right next door.

The three of us rolled out of bed and onto the floor, then looked up at each other in disbelief. Ten shots. Then twenty. Then twenty more. In our part of town, nighttime gunfire was as common as hearing the cats fighting outside our dorm windows or the shopping carts being pushed along the cracked sidewalk in front of the firehouse. But almost always it was the sound of handguns. Residents figured popping off a few rounds into the night sky was as good a way to celebrate as anything else, or as good a way to scare off intruders as anything else. Hearing something bigger than a 9mm or a .38 special was rare. And normally gunfire associated with a crime would mean a shot or two followed by squealing tires.

Not this time. There was a war going on outside, and it didn't take a four-star general to figure out who was doing the shooting—or who was being shot. We knew we'd be sprinting directly toward the biker warehouse the second our brothers in blue from OPD rendered the scene safe.

The gunfire lasted maybe a minute. As soon as the last shot faded, the night was shattered by a new set of sounds.

Shouts. Screams. Fists banging on the apparatus bay. Wailing.

We sat tight in the dorm and waited. It sounds heartless, but firefighters aren't paid to stop crime. If we arrived on the scene of a gun battle *before* OPD, we would risk becoming victims ourselves.

Cappy hollered over from the officer's bedroom, "You all good in there?"

"We're good," Rog yelled back. "How 'bout you?"

Cappy laughed. "Besides wetting myself, yeah, I'm good!"

We all chuckled. He knew how to diffuse stress in a bad situation and get us ready to roll. I listened hard and soon was tracking the incoming sirens racing down what I knew was Thirty-Second Street and then turning on MLK. Ten seconds later came the welcome roar of three OPD squad cars accelerating past our firehouse, their throttles pegged and lights strobing through our dorm windows.

"Alright, boys," yelled Cappy, "let's get to work!"

—◇—

Two minutes later we were on scene. As firefighters our main objective was always patient care and safety. Usually, if it was a crime scene, we'd do our best not to contaminate the evidence.

Not this time. There were so many shell casings on the ground outside the main entrance that I almost slipped like a cartoon character on a banana peel. I caught my balance. *Screw this*, I thought, then jogged inside, shuffling my feet and scattering what seemed like hundreds of tinkling casings in front of me. There was a short hallway, and then I popped into the main warehouse space. The air was thick with smoke, and the orange industrial lighting overhead gave the entire room a sick glow. The only sound was an unearthly screaming coming from one of the victims.

Oakland Police were already doing whatever police stuff needed doing. Some were fanned out, guns drawn. Others were examining the ground or trying to question victims. None of the victims had on biker vests, and I couldn't see any weapons. Chances were, whoever did the shooting had taken both to cover their tracks.

I scanned the room. *One, two, three, four victims.* I scanned again. Same count. We'd need backup, pronto. Each victim would need two firefighters for treatment, and that's if the injuries weren't severe. And with the amount of lead that had been flying around, there was no way the injuries weren't severe. Cappy was in charge of the scene like always, but as paramedic, I was the highest-ranking medical provider. I knew he would deliver whatever I needed.

"Cappy, get us two more ambulances and another engine company!" I shouted.

He keyed up his mic and called in my request, then took up position where he could see the whole room. His job was to keep his head on a swivel and make sure me, Jimmy, and Rog could do our jobs.

Triage time. With too few emergency responders on scene, we were going to have to be ruthless.

I hit my knees beside victim one. "Hey, bro, how you feeling?" I asked cheerfully as I pulled up his shirt. He was flat on his back in a rapidly expanding pool of blood underneath him. There was an entry wound in the middle of his chest. His face was covered in beads of sweat, and he was breathing—or trying to breathe—a mile a minute. No way he was going to make it. I glanced back at Cappy, who was standing nearby. He did a little thing where he clenched the corner of his mouth. I recognized his meaning. He agreed with me. *Goner.* I patted the victim's arm. "Hold tight, bro, I'll be right back."

I moved as quickly as I could to victim two, but before I even reached him, I turned toward victim three. My Sherlock-level deduction skills told me to move on, since half of victim two's head was missing.

Victim three, a female, was the one who'd been screaming. Now she was silent and going into shock. Jimmy was already at her side and Rog was jogging up. She'd taken two bullets, one through the stomach and one in her upper left thigh. Or what *had* been her thigh. That leg was practically amputated. Bone and bits of muscle cratered her leather pants. Her femoral artery had to have been hit, which meant she was on a five-minute countdown to bleeding out, and that wasn't even considering her abdominal wound.

"Jimmy, throw a tourniquet on her leg just above that femur that's poking out," I yelled.

"I know, I know," he snapped, opening his kit. "On it!"

"I know you know. Just get that bleeding stopped!"

I jammed a large-bore IV into her jugular and got a bag of normal saline flowing to replace the blood she'd lost and was continuing to lose. "Rog, pressure the stomach shot and get her oxygen!"

Jimmy and Rog would have their hands full attempting to pull off what the victim needed, but I was already moving on to victim four. Just the way it had to be. This guy was bleeding from a shot to the right shoulder. Nothing critical, probably, but he was still losing a lot of blood. I helped him scootch back and sit up against the nearest wall to slow the bleeding. Then I yanked a bandage out of my kit and instructed him to push it as tight as possible against the wound.

"Help's coming soon," I told him. "Just hang on."

Four, three, two, one. Second round of triage. Since Jimmy and Rog were with victim three and more help was on the way for victim four, I raced back to victim one. The pool of blood was now completely surrounding him. He'd be gone any second, but as long as he was still with us, I needed to give him everything I had. Kneeling beside him, I looked again at the entry point on his chest. Every time he gasped for air, his wound sprayed air and blood in a tiny geyser. I pulled out a sealed dressing and slapped it over the wound. Tears were running down the corners of his eyes every time he blinked.

"Hey, bud," I said lightly, "got your bleeding stopped. Now let's get you stabilized."

I noticed he was using his remaining strength to reach into his pocket and attempt to pull something out. To ensure he wasn't going for a weapon, I eased his hand out of the way and reached in. I pulled out a vibrating cell phone. I looked at the screen. Block letters told me the tale: MOM.

I lifted his hand and put the cell phone into his palm, wondering if he could answer. His fingers strained, and I heard the *beep* of an accepted call. Somehow he managed to get the cell all the way to his ear. His hand started to shake bad enough that I gripped his wrist and held it steady.

I could barely hear a Charlie Brown–teacher voice on the other end. But all he could do for an answer was gasp and gasp. More tears poured from the corners of his eyes. As a caring human, I wanted to assist him and hold the phone so he could listen to the person on the other end. But I knew who was on the other end—and as a seasoned paramedic, I didn't want the woman's last memories of her son to be his gasping for air as he died. So I used my other hand to end the call. His arm collapsed beside his head, and the phone clattered onto the concrete, its lower half resting in the pool of blood.

I grabbed "the bag" from my kit, fitted it over his face, and started to breathe for him, one breath every five seconds or so.

Two breaths in, the victim's phone lit up again: MOM. It vibrated, sending ripples into the pool of blood. I wanted to pick up the phone more than I'd wanted almost anything before. But it was just me, and I had one hand holding the face mask to his face and the other squeezing the bag. I gritted my teeth and watched the phone.

The man convulsed, then stopped breathing. The phone went dark. I dropped my bag and looked up. Third round of triage.

I stood and jogged toward Jimmy and Rog, who were still with the woman. Shoulder guy had an ambulance crew with him. Cappy must have directed them over while I was with the dying man. I reached the woman just as a second ambulance crew ran in pushing a gurney. With Jimmy and Rog helping, they did a load-and-go, lifting the victim onto the wheeled bed and heading outside. Jimmy and Rog followed to help with patient care on the way to the trauma center.

And just like that it was over. It was just me, Cappy, and two dozen cops left on scene.

I had thirty minutes of paperwork any time I declared victims dead on scene. When that was finished, we'd head up to the hospital to grab our guys.

I glanced back at the body of victim one. There was still a layer of smoke hanging over the floor like ground fog.

And when the smoke lit, I knew who was still trying to call him.

When I was a boy my mom was my world.

"You weren't even supposed to be born," she used to tell me.

"That's why you're my special boy. The doctor told me you'd never be born, you'd never survive. But here you are. My special, special boy."

When my parents divorced, she moved away, and I stayed with my dad. She asked me to come live with her a few times and I gave it a shot a few times. When Mom wasn't around, though, her roommates or boyfriends were, and all of them made it very clear that kids were just burdens on the lives of adults. And each time I made an attempt to try to start a new life with her, Dad would visit and find a way to convince me to move back to his place.

Whatever. They'd both tried their best—were trying their best—but they'd been too hurt themselves to know what I needed. My decision about which parent to live with didn't really matter that much. Mom and Dad were looking for good lives for themselves. But whatever that meant for them, it wasn't what I wanted.

So when I was old enough I just sort of . . . checked out. Like checking out from a hotel, except I left my family.

The morning after the warehouse shooting I looked through the paper. It said there had been two fatalities and two victims were in critical condition at the hospital. After chatting with the incoming shift, I trudged to my truck in the firehouse lot, ready to head home and count the minutes until my next shift. I didn't know or care what day it was. It was just time to get home and back to my normal routine of surviving, hour by hour.

My fingers were on the key, ready to start the engine, when I shivered. Paused. I heard the exact same voice from the morning Chad called for waffles, and it was telling me to do something.

What is it with being in your truck that makes you get all weird, Sautel?

But this time the voice got even weirder. It told me I *wanted* to do something I didn't want to do. Which made no sense. With a sigh I told the voice to stop pestering me and that I'd do what it told me to in just a minute.

I fired up my truck and pulled onto the street. As soon as I was on Interstate 880, I dialed my mom. It had been a few months since we'd talked. Last time had been when I'd broken it off with another girl and she had wanted to give me some advice.

"Really?" I'd said. "*You're* going to give *me* relationship advice? Cute!"

The call had gone downhill from there.

She'd tried calling back a few times that week, but I realized I didn't need to send any more of my pain her way. So I did what I always did and checked out.

I heard the call connect.

"Jason!" she answered on the third ring. "What a wonderful surprise to hear from my son. And on Mother's Day too!"

CHAPTER 11

ALONE

IT WAS A WARM evening, and the four of us were joking around behind the firehouse. Jimmy had just returned from vacationing in Cabo, with some of the guys from another station no less. He was one of those guys who always had a hookup or an inside line on something cool: concert tickets, a killer deal on a used 4x4, or, in this case, an all-inclusive resort for next to nothing.

Once we let him know what a jerk he was for going to Mexico without us, we suggested that all might be forgiven if he'd brought us any presents.

"Guys, guys, *of course* I got you something," he assured us. He was a smooth one. So smooth I almost believed him. "And not just any old present either. I got *Cohibas*. You're lucky I like you all so much."

I knew there was no chance Jimmy had sprung for such good cigars, and on the off chance he had, there was no way he'd waste any on us. "Cohibas, huh?" I smirked, then reached into my pocket and grabbed a pack of grape-flavored Swisher Sweets I'd picked up for two bucks at the Kwik-E-Mart. I opened the package and handed one to

Cappy. "If Jimmy brought real Cubans," I said, "then these right here are Romeo y Julietas!"

Rog and Cappy busted up, but Jimmy had other ideas. While I laughed and tried to light my Swisher, he did his best to subdue me with a chokehold and shove one of his "Cohibas" in my mouth.

But dispatch was still loud enough to hear over the sound of our horseplay. When the fire call came in, we froze and listened to the conversation.

"Ma'am, where is the fire?"

"Right next door to me! On seven hundred block of thirty-fifth street. Hurry!"

That was pretty close. We raced to the engine, and Rog and Cappy ran to the map on the far wall. Amazingly, it was hand-drawn, made back in the sixties by some guy with a photographic memory. And even more amazingly, it showed every hydrant location in our entire district.

Cappy squinted for a second and then whacked a location on the map with the back of his hand. "Rog, you're gonna catch *this* hydrant. If it's dead, here's your secondary."

Our engine carried 500 gallons of water, which sounds like a lot, except we'd push 125 gallons per *minute* on a raging fire. Without an accessible hydrant we'd be toast—and so would the structure.

Soon we roared out of the firehouse, and I stood up to look forward. With the wind trying its best to rip my cigar out of my mouth, I took a couple more puffs, smashed it up against the chest of my turnout coat to extinguish it, and tossed it into the street. I'd barely smoked it, so it would be a good find for one of the homeless folks wandering the street that night.

Cappy, riding shotgun, spotted the plume of smoke first. He hollered back, "We got one, boys!"

My nerves spiked the instant I recognized the block. I'd been here before, and it was 100 percent Victorians. Wood, of course, like the day they were first built, but when you mixed in cheap synthetic sofas, carpet made from who-knows-what, and electronics gear, you were looking at a potentially nasty situation. Not to mention every single house was within literal spitting distance of the next one, and hungry fire just loved to jump little gaps as it hunted for its next meal. If we didn't knock down the fire in this Vicky exactly the right way, we might be having to explain why an entire block of the city was missing.

To top off the challenge, Victorians were more complicated than single-story fires because they had balloon frames that reached from the foundation all the way to the attic. That meant there were no fire stops in the walls, so a basement fire could quickly run right up and get the attic rolling! Plus, most had a ton of square footage, leaving plenty of space for what might be considered "creative" housing arrangements. Who would bother to notify the great city of Oakland if they subdivided three rooms on the second story, built a rickety external staircase, and then rented the rooms out in cash to the boyfriend of their cousin's ex-girlfriend?

When we arrived, I could see the fire raging in the basement. Flames were pouring out from two dirt-level windows on the right side of the house.

"Seed!" Cappy yelled as Rog stopped and switched the engine into pump mode. "It's in the basement!"

"Got it, Cappy!" I yelled, jumping down.

A less seasoned fire officer might have instructed us about what diameter of hose to grab and how much, but Cappy knew we knew our jobs. I grabbed 150 feet of pre-connected hose with a nozzle attached out of the hose bed closest to the burning Vicky. I slung one hundred feet over my shoulder, and the remaining fifty feet uncoiled between me and the engine as I leaned into my run toward the basement door. Cappy slotted in behind me as I advanced. Jimmy had already sprinted to the metal ground-level security door to force it open with a flathead ax and a halligan bar, which was basically an overpowered cat's paw that pulled out entire door hinges instead of just bent nails.

I powered toward Jimmy, letting hose flake off my shoulder along the way. I noticed there were bars on almost all the windows. Understandable in this neighborhood, but in an active fire, those safety measures could become deadly. By the time we reached the security door, Jimmy had pried it open and chocked it with a wooden wedge. Every door we opened got chocked without exception, because if a door closed behind us as we were advancing into a fire or searching for victims, there could be fatal consequences. Behind the security door was a wooden door to the basement. Jimmy tested the doorknob with his gloved hand. He looked back and nodded, which meant it was unlocked. He left it closed while we got the water ready.

I dropped to my knees in front of the door, with Cappy and Jimmy nearby. Rog ran to a spot where we could make eye contact and yelled, "Water?!" It was a question, not an order. He'd never send water until we asked for it—150 pounds of pressure charging into an unattended hose line could do a lot of damage to an unsuspecting nozzle team.

I yelled, "Water!" loud enough for someone three blocks away to hear and swung my right hand in a circular motion above my head.

Rog confirmed my order by yelling back, "Water coming!" as he waved his arm. Radios are cute, but old-school eye contact and screaming were our modus operandi. He disappeared to the pump panel.

While keeping my knee on the hose and waiting the five seconds for the water to arrive, I pulled on the mask that was attached to the bottle on my back. Then I grabbed the nozzle and heard the characteristic sound of air being pushed out as the flattened hose quickly filled, snaking its way up the driveway.

I nodded at Jimmy, and he pushed the door open. The three of us prepared to advance, getting as low as we could so we wouldn't get cooked by the initial blast of trapped heat as it rapidly escaped.

Most people are used to thinking of fire on a different scale than firefighters. Fire in a fireplace or a campfire ring can feel hot but also cozy. An oven might burn you, but it probably won't *burn* you. When you fight fire, though, you're getting up close and personal with flames that are unimaginably hot. Out of all the unimaginably hot fires, basement fires might just be the suckiest. Not only does a basement's low ceiling trap every bit of heat closer to the floor, but just to get into most basements the firefighters need to descend through a chimney of absolute pain. The second you vent a basement fire by opening the stairwell, all that pent-up heat gets it in its mind to move up to airier pastures. And you're in its way.

But none of that changed our actions. We had to get into that subterranean inferno as quick as we could, both to save anyone trapped below and to keep the rest of the house from igniting. Jimmy and Cappy were right behind me, Cappy helping to pull the hose line and Jimmy carrying the tools we might need in case we came upon any more doors blocking our advance. But all three of us were going to be trapped in that pain chimney until I got us onto the ever-so-slightly-less-terrible basement floor.

I plowed down the entry stairs like the devil was chasing me. A few steps down, my neck and ears blistered. Halfway down, the blisters on my neck and ears started to get their own adorable baby blisters. Ten seconds in, I hit what I *thought* was the basement floor—except it was just a landing with more steps on the other side. I tumbled forward, down the second set of stairs and into the blackness, simultaneously dropping the hose and pondering the popping noise in my ankle. As quick as the pain came, so did a jolt of adrenaline, putting the pain right to sleep. Two seconds later I'd gotten myself back up to the landing with Cappy and Jimmy.

"Damn, bro," Jimmy yelled through his mask. "Thought you were gone! Here!" He handed me the nozzle I'd dropped, and I immediately moved down past the final bit of the stairway. I landed on my belly on the basement floor and commando-crawled forward. Then Cappy and Jimmy hit the floor behind me. We'd made it past the red-hot stairway, and I sighed in relief at the mild 500-degree air.

The three of us slithered on our bellies across the basement floor. We needed to find the seat of the fire. In the pitch dark, we trusted our instincts: hotter and louder meant we were getting closer. *There.* A glow to our left. I crawled toward it but pulled up short. A familiar burning sensation was spreading across my body—forearms, elbows, abs, thighs. I was crawling across melting carpet, aka freakish chemicals heated to a liquid state. I focused the nozzle on the ground and opened it up until I was sure the carpet was mostly steaming water before continuing toward the glow.

Around and above us I could hear windows being smashed by the arriving crews. We never ventilated until a hose line was in place—but once a hose line was there, the next crew would pop the windows to let the superheated air escape. That meant we could soon stand up but also that the building would be "free burning," since we were feeding the fire copious amounts of its favorite food: oxygen.

Then over the noise of breaking glass and roaring flames came the screech of the metal saws ripping through security bars on every basement and ground-floor window. If things got hairy for us unexpectedly and we needed to bail, it would suck to reach a house window only to discover that it was actually a jail window.

Suddenly a dangerous redness rolled above us as we pushed forward. Glancing up, I saw flames oozing along the ceiling. They were seconds from igniting the floor joists above us and taking the first story. I rolled onto my side, then back, aiming the nozzle up to darken them down. The patter of water and ash hitting my face mask and lid grew loud. Then I rolled back, slithering forward toward the orange glow pumping its heat our way.

Finally, we reached the seat of the fire. We rose to our knees. Thankfully the visibility was getting better as some of the heat and smoke vented through the windows. Best I could tell, we were in a makeshift bedroom. I opened up the nozzle again. With 125 gallons per minute surging through, the fire began to darken. I swung the nozzle in a clockwise pattern, hitting the ceiling and letting the water violently rain down as it continued to stomp the life out of old man fire.

As the water soaked every surface, I could finally begin to see the room properly. Steam was sucking out through the broken windows, and a small amount of light from the streetlights and emergency lights was filtering in. With my flashlight—which had been clipped on me the whole time, completely worthless in the thick, black smoke—I could finally scan the room. The sound of another crew's axes above let me know some fire had worked its way into at least one wall. They'd be chasing it down and killing it.

The first thing I saw was a bed. The second was a large object on the bed. The bed and the object were still smoldering. I hit both with my nozzle, desperately wanting the object to be just that—a thing, not a person.

Water dripped. Ash settled. More smoke cleared. And I was staring at what had been a person. It was obvious he'd been sleeping when the fire started. He'd never even had a chance to escape his bed. The body was well over six feet and three hundred pounds. I felt Cappy put a hand on my shoulder. He was seeing what I was seeing. Then I heard him radio the battalion chief outside, "One deceased victim in the basement. Notify the coroner."

We continued to work the fire. None of us would be leaving before the low-air alarm on our bottles went off. Leave early with extra air, and you'd get a reputation as a lump, a slacker. We were workers, not lumps, and every other station knew it. By the time my bottle chimed, there were eight or ten responders in the basement, all of us hitting hot spots and making sure nothing could reignite.

Cappy patted me on the back. "Come on, Seed. Let's step out and ditch these bottles for some fresh air."

By the time we made it back to the basement steps, the pain in my ankle had woken up, and man, was it pissed off about missing the action. I stopped to stretch, while Cappy and Jimmy made their way past me up the stairs. Before starting to climb, I looked back toward the basement bedroom. With my flashlight it was still possible to see the shape of the victim lying on his bed.

I tried to swallow. Usually when I couldn't reach a victim in time, I'd feel a punch of guilty regret in my gut. This time, looking at this body, I felt something different. Sadness. Fear mixed with sadness. He'd died all alone, surrounded by people, but trapped in a personal hell of darkness and pain. *You can't go out that way, Sautel. You can't stay so alone.*

I turned and climbed the same set of stairs that just minutes before had been a chimney of death. Step, step, landing. I yanked off my helmet, then my face mask. Step, step, step, and I could hear shouting in the front yard. My ankle felt like someone had stabbed it with a steak knife. Fresh, cool air at last. I set down my helmet and mask, then pulled off my bottle and coat, and looked around. The scene in the driveway had been repeated countless times in our city alone. There was a woman inside the perimeter of yellow caution tape.

"Where's James?" she asked franticly. "Did James make it?" As the later-arriving crews went about their business, she jogged from person to person, asking and not getting an answer.

Then Cappy made his way to her and got her attention. He shook his head no.

She half collapsed, grabbing for Cappy's shoulder, as a low moan became a long, agonized wailing.

Cappy, plastered in soot and grime, scanned the bystanders on the other side of the yellow tape and motioned for two of them to come across the line and console the woman. Soon a blanket was wrapped around the woman's shuddering shoulders, and friendly arms held her tight.

She began to breathe more normally and then began to tell the story of James.

The deceased man had moved into the basement of his own house twenty years before. His wife and daughter had left him because of his drinking problem, and he couldn't face living in the same rooms that held their ghosts. He'd quit drinking the day he chose the basement and had never gone back to the bottle. His wife and daughter never returned, but he never rented out the upper stories because he never stopped hoping.

"He was retired," the woman said, "but he was always workin', you know? He'd be the first to carry someone's groceries, the first to fix someone's broken step, the first to be down in the dirt in someone's yard that ain't even his own, pullin' weeds that ain't even his own." She started to cry again. "We called him James the gentle giant. All us neighbors called him that. The gentle giant."

His story was killing me. I spun and walked back down into the basement. The first thing that hit my nostrils was the unmistakable odor of a burned human being. Water drip-drip-dripped from the ceiling. I limped to the bedside to say goodbye. *Twenty years down here. Twenty years alone. Goodbye, James, the gentle giant.*

Just then, something in the room attached itself to me. I felt it cling like it had talons. I forced myself to breathe normally so I could pay attention to what I was experiencing. Then the words came to name it. *I know what it feels like to die alone.*

I stood in front of James and pictured myself on my bed. Pictured my own death. I wanted something different than the isolation of this man. I *needed* something different—but where could I find it? Two minutes earlier I'd been staring at a burned corpse. Nothing more, nothing less. I lost track of how many dead bodies I'd seen over the years. I treated every deceased victim with respect, but they were still just bodies. But now this body had a name, a history—and

I understood that he was me. That I was suffering the same fate, just with the film running on a slower speed.

The goodbye took only a moment. Soon the coroner would arrive, but we weren't going to be sitting around waiting for him. We'd start in on the backbreaking work of tearing the basement apart and removing anything that had been touched by fire.

Except for James.

We'd be working around him until the coroner arrived. And then we'd help lift what was left of James into the body bag and clear out the burned-out shell of the bed where he'd started his eternal nap.

A couple of hours passed before we finished, and I forced my ankle up the basement steps again. Outside, a few neighbors were still rehashing stories about the fire and James. I wondered what my neighbors would say about me. I knew the answer. *He seemed like a nice guy. Kept a neat house. Kind of a loner but smiled and waved if you waved at him first.*

But even that shallow summary was a lie. The real me was as hidden from the rest of the world as James the gentle giant had been during the fire. I knew what James had felt: isolation, terror, sadness, agony.

I craved the opposite. I needed antidotes. But since when did it matter what I wanted?

As always, I was locked in a pit of pain with no way to call for rescue.

CHAPTER 12

HOUSE OF LOVE

WE FOUND THE OLD man in his bed, motionless on top of the covers. He was flat on his back, hands folded on his chest, legs straight ahead, eyes closed. He looked peaceful.

The lines around his wife's mouth and eyes betrayed her fear. So did the white handkerchief she kept twisted tight in her hands. Still, she spoke calmly to Cappy. Her husband hadn't felt well after lunch, so he'd gone into his room to take an afternoon nap, telling her a bit of rest before dinner would set him right. Then he gave her a kiss and walked down the hallway to their bedroom.

"Almost seventy," she told Cappy, "almost seventy years we've been married."

I moved quickly to the man's side and subtly checked for a pulse while Cappy listened. When he glanced at me, I gave him a small head shake.

Cappy put a gentle hand on the wife's shoulder. "Let's go into the living room so I can ask you some questions about his medical history," he invited, "and we'll give my guys a bit of space."

The woman's blue-and-white flowered dress flared as she turned and followed Cappy into the hallway. He let her pass and then shut the door.

The minute the door closed, Jimmy and Rog moved the man onto the floor to begin CPR. He'd almost certainly suffered a massive heart attack, and CPR would keep his blood circulating until we could confirm either that his heart had restarted or that we could stop resuscitative efforts. Our chances were slim, but not zero. Rog yanked open the front of the man's button-up shirt, and Jimmy cut a ragged strip down the front of the man's undershirt, exposing his chest. I started an IV and inserted a breathing tube down his throat, then fastened the electrodes from my monitor onto the man's bare chest. *Beeeeeeeeeee.* Asystole. Flatline. Just like my fingertips had told me earlier.

Rog and Jimmy took two-minute shifts, with one performing the chest compressions and the other working the airway bag. Cake job was the airway: two squeezes on the bag at the end of every thirty compressions. The rough stuff was pushing down on a human rib cage with enough force to circulate blood. Real CPR is torture. What makes it okay is that it's a few ticks down the torture scale from death.

"One, two, three . . ." Rog counted out his pushes.

I prepared a one-milligram injection of epinephrine to push into the IV. I listened to the old man's ribs popping and cracking with each violent compression.

". . . twenty-eight, twenty-nine, thirty."

Jimmy squeezed the bag twice. Then Rog took the bag and Jimmy began compressions. The three of us had danced this sad song so many times we knew the steps by heart.

Between epinephrine injections, I looked around the room. He was a military man. Everything about the room and its contents made perfect sense, from the neatly pleated bedding to the pressed slacks hanging in the closet below matching pressed shirts. House slippers peeked out from the foot of the bed. On the nightstand was a silver-framed picture of the man and his beautiful bride on their wedding day. He wore his dress uniform, she a simple white gown. They stood on a dirt road, hand in hand, near the steps of a small wooden church.

Jimmy and Rog switched again. I pushed a second round of epinephrine. "Be right back," I told them.

The hallway was like a museum dedicated to true love. Picture frame after picture frame marching through the decades. The man and the woman were always smiling.

Cappy was speaking with the woman when I reached the living room. "That's when we called 911," she was telling him, "and then you came."

The room felt like a Hallmark movie set in the 1950s. Two chintz wing chairs faced the hearth, and between them a small table, where a folded newspaper, reading glasses, and an enormous leather Bible sat on doilies.

Cappy saw me coming and excused himself from the woman. "Lemme talk to my guy a second," he said, "and then I'll be right back with you."

I lowered my head, and we turned away from her. "History?" I asked.

"Clean as a whistle," he reported. "Just a single prescription for blood pressure."

My eyebrows popped.

"I know," Cappy agreed. "Hope we're that healthy at ninety. Any—"

"They're still working," I said. He knew what that meant. I turned back toward the hallway when the woman called out.

"How is my beloved?"

"Ma'am, we're doing everything they would do at the hospital," I said quickly, avoiding her eyes, "but as of now his heart's still not beating on its own."

Cappy stepped toward her. I knew he'd explain some of what we were doing in an attempt to keep her mind occupied. I walked down the hall as quickly as I could and reentered the bedroom.

Fifteen minutes later I called it. "Stop CPR, fellas."

The heart monitor had never moved from flatline. Even if his heart started now—impossible, but even if—it would be pointless. His brain had been without oxygen for way too long. I looked at the metal alarm clock on the bedside table and mentally noted the time of death to tell the coroner. Standard procedure was to leave in place any IVs, breathing tubes, and electrodes. Typically, the coroner would remove them at the county morgue, but I didn't expect the coroner to respond to this scene. An OPD officer would show up to take a report anytime we pronounced someone dead on scene, and since it was so clear that this gentleman had died of natural causes, they would take a quick report from me and then radio the coroner that he wasn't needed.

"Guys?" I asked. Rog and Jimmy knew what was up. They eased the lifeless man into a sitting position. Rog supported the man's torso while I cut away the rest of his shirt and undershirt and crumpled both into our biohazard bag. Next I removed the breathing tube, electrodes, and IV line, placing a bandage over the tiny bloom of blood. Meanwhile, Jimmy had selected a fresh white shirt from the closet. Together we dressed the man, buttoning his clean shirt and tucking it neatly into his slacks. Then we lifted him back onto his bed, arranging his body just as it had been when we arrived. I reached out and brushed my fingers through his thin hair, right to left across his forehead and downward above his ears. I wanted him to look the same as when he'd kissed his wife before his nap.

Rog had his head bowed in what I could tell was one of his silent prayers. Instead of poking his ribs to annoy him like I usually did, I said quietly to Jimmy, "I'll go tell her." He nodded.

In my heavy work boots, I sounded like an elephant tromping down the hallway past their family photographs. The woman was waiting for me in the living room. Her handkerchief was gone, and now she held the Bible I'd seen on the table.

She spoke before I could. "My love is with Jesus, isn't he?"

I nodded yes, then looked away. My lower lip and chin began to quiver, so I clamped my teeth tight. *What are you doing, Sautel? You're sad, yeah, but why are you confirming her fairy tale?*

She turned and walked toward the twin chairs. She set the Bible down softly on the small table and straightened it. Then she turned back toward me and opened her arms wide. I found myself wrapped in her embrace.

"I'm sorry," I mumbled. She was all of five feet, four inches, and maybe a hundred pounds.

She turned her head sideways against my chest, and as if I were one of her own, she said in a soft and eloquent southern accent, "Child, child, child, it's not your fault."

"I'm sorry," I said again.

She tightened her arms around me. "You know God called him home?"

"Yes," I found myself agreeing, "yes, he did."

What was happening? I wondered how she could have so much extra love that she tossed it around without considering the consequences. Her husband had just died, and she was comforting *me*. No, her *world* had just ended, and she was comforting me. She'd spent her entire adult life loving the man I'd just pronounced dead, and now she was pulling me into her arms and forgiving me for not saving him.

The church down the road had turned me away because of what I was wearing. But it seemed like this old woman was accepting me *because* of what I was wearing.

As a paramedic I'd tried to save her husband—and failed. Now it was me hurting, and her turn to try and save someone. I closed my eyes and let her hug me. Those few seconds felt like they lasted forever, and I didn't want them to end.

CHAPTER 13

GIRL TIME

I **WAS STRAIGHT TRIPPING** when dispatch announced a structure fire at 5:30 a.m.

Not because of the fire. It didn't sound like anything too rough. But I had a morning appointment I could *not* miss, and the fire meant I was going to have to cut things way too close.

By the time we knocked down the fire and drove back to the station, it was already 7:30 a.m. I jumped off the engine before it had fully stopped and sprinted to put my gear away and clean up the tools we'd used.

"Yo, Seed," yelled Rog. "Leave that alone. We got you. Now go get that little niece of yours!"

I nodded a quick thanks, raced to take a one-minute shower, practically jumped into a pair of board shorts and a faded T-shirt, topped my outfit with a backward OFD cap, ran to my truck, and burned rubber out of the parking lot.

The dashboard clock read 7:38 a.m. *Way* too close.

———◇———

The stress was pumping as I charged through the airport. Maybe I should have taken the extra minute to pull on some running shoes, because my flip-flops were not helping me make up for lost time. *Slap, slap, slap.*

I wanted to shout, "Outta my way!" but it wasn't really an OFD emergency. I was just under strict orders from my sister to be at Gate 18 at the San Francisco International Airport no later than 9:30 a.m. to pick up Bethany, who was flying out from North Carolina to spend the week with me.

Between dodging bros carrying surfboard bags, parents dragging way too much luggage and way too many kids, and all the folks rattling cans and asking for donations, I could have used a portable siren. No one was giving me the space I clearly deserved.

My sister and I hadn't really grown up together, and we'd never been close, but I connected with Bethany. When I was around her, I felt like I had a sense of purpose that didn't involve fighting fire or rescuing people.

This was the first time Bethany was coming to visit me, instead of the other way around, and my sister made it exceedingly clear that if I was late to pick up her precious unaccompanied minor, there would be hell to pay. *Slap, slap, slap.* I could see the TSA line ahead. I couldn't remember my sister's exact words—something involving "don't you dare be late" and "feel my wrath"—but I remembered the tone of her voice. She wasn't messing around.

I finally slid to a halt at the security line, which was mercifully empty. I pulled out my wallet and grabbed the form that would let me—and only me—pick up Bethany at the gate. Then I tossed my wallet, keys, and flip-flops in one of the baskets and pushed it into the X-ray machine. *C'mon, c'mon, c'mon,* I urged the X-ray belt. *Move faster.* Then the belt stopped. I glanced up to find the tech looking at me.

"Sir, I'm gonna ask you to step over here," he told me. With that, he advanced the belt and handed the basket to his coworker.

Seriously? I wasn't going to create a scene, but I absolutely had to get going! *Okay, Sautel, de-escalate.* "No prob, guys," I responded, looking at the two of them in turn. Then I gave my best smile and said, "You know, I'm not below bribes every so often. How about twenty bucks for each of you?"

The only laugh came from the woman waiting behind me. Meanwhile, the officers I'd mentally labeled Stilts and Neckbeard gave me the good ol' "we are not amused" face that every government lackey learns on day one of training.

"Yeah, you're going to have to stay with us," said Stilts, "for at least a *bit* longer."

"But I—"

"Sir," interrupted Neckbeard, "are you aware it is a violation of federal law to attempt to bring a weapon through airport security?"

A weapon? I didn't have any . . . Oh, no freaking way.

They were detaining me because of my OFD wallet badge. I carried my badge whenever I was off duty—along with every other sworn member of the OFD and OPD—in case we happened upon an emergency on our days off. And the so-called weapon? An inch-and-a-half-long straight pin that I used to fasten the badge inside my wallet. Had these guys' houses just burned down or something?

I dropped the smile and tried to bro it up a bit. "Okay. I'm going to break something down for you," I began, alternating my stare between Neckbeard and Stilts, which probably looked more like crazy eyes. But I continued, "I'm late to pick up my niece, who is *eleven*, and you're going to stand there and tell me I can't do that because you think a city badge with a pin is a motherf—"

"Gentlemen!" The voice that interrupted me came from a San Francisco police officer who had just arrived. I turned from the TSA bozos and gave him a once-over. Perfectly ironed uniform, shined shoes, and a patch from Operation Desert Storm. I decided to shut up and wait.

The officer looked me over and then stuck out his hand toward Stilts, who handed him my wallet. He flipped it open and looked inside. "Oakland Fire?" he asked me.

"Yes, sir!" I answered. "And I gotta be at Gate 18 like yesterday to grab my little niece!"

He nodded at me, then looked at the TSA guys, and nodded toward the gate area. "Here's your wallet back."

It took me about ten seconds to wriggle my toes into my flip-flops, clap the officer on the shoulder, say, "Thanks, bro," and resume my sprint.

I weaved and slap-slap-slapped my way past Gate 10, 12, 14 . . . *Yes!* I could see Gate 18, and the door from the jetway had just opened. I stopped my mad dash and tried to catch my breath as I watched the gate agent lean over to adjust one of the elastic-fence supports. She was older and was struggling with the connection, so I gave her a hand. She thanked me and said she had more work for me if I needed a job. I started to answer, but then walking through the door was a flight attendant holding the hand of the most beautiful child I'd ever seen. Bethany was wearing a blue and green sundress. The second she saw me she pulled her hand away from the flight attendant and ran toward me. Her curly brown hair bounced around the edges of her glasses, and then all of a sudden she was in my arms, squeezing the breath out of me.

I felt a lump in my throat, but not the usual kind made of dread and loneliness. This one was made of goodness, which struck me dumb. Here was someone who looked up to me. Who didn't worry about my flaws and faults. I hugged her back and successfully blinked away a few tears before the flight attendant arrived.

"Let me guess," she said, giving me an appraising look, "Uncle Jason the fireman?"

"Yes, ma'am."

"Well, Jason, your niece spent the entire flight talking about you. She has some interesting ideas about why you're still single. Don't you, Bethany?"

Uh-oh, Sautel, what have you gotten yourself into?

The flight attendant continued. "She *also* told me that you were looking for a single flight attendant. After she asked me if I was married or not, that is." She held up her left ring finger, which was bare. I finally paid attention to her. She was gorgeous. "Unfortunately," she concluded, "I live on the East Coast, so Miss Bethany is going to have to keep searching for an aunt."

My niece grinned and nodded. The flight attendant laughed. Then they looked at each other and laughed some more. I just stood there with my mouth open like a big dummy.

⬦

That night, Bethany and I met my mom for dinner at a Mexican joint in Santa Rosa. La Cantina was hopping with a mix of families, singles, and students from Sonoma State. Up to that point in my life, I'd spent way too many hours hanging out at the bar, which stayed open long after the restaurant closed down, but I hadn't spent much time in the restaurant.

The hostess showed us to a table and said our server would be along soon. I was content to listen to Mom and Bethany chat while powering my way through the chips and salsa. I was on chip basket two and salsa cup three when . . . well, there's no way else to put it: I found myself living every romantic cliché simultaneously.

I looked up and saw a server at another table. Time stood still. My jaw hit the floor, and at the same time she took my breath away. She was radiant. It was love at first sight. I was on cloud nine.

When the server floated back toward the kitchen, a bit of salsa slid down my chin and onto my lap. I looked back to my mom and niece to see if they saw what I saw. I tried to swallow but couldn't. I reached for a chip, and my hand was shaking. *Come on, Sautel!* I grabbed my menu just in time to nearly drop it when the server came to our table.

"Hi, I'm Kristie," said the glowing, gorgeous voice, "and I'll be taking care of you guys tonight. Can I get you something to drink?"

I looked down at my menu. Why were all the words spinning in circles?

"I'll have a Shirley Temple," Bethany piped up.

Mom ordered an iced tea.

Uh-oh. I gripped the menu even tighter. "Beer," I managed. *Slick, Sautel. Real slick.*

"What kind? We've got—"

"Corona!" I almost shouted, interrupting her before she could recite the list.

"Okay, sounds good," Kristie said, smiling at all of us. It was more like she'd sung it. Like an angel was singing to me. "I'll be back soon."

The second she left, Bethany kicked me in the shin—*hard*—under the table. I snapped my attention back to her.

"Uncle Jason, don't stare!" she said seriously. Then she broke into a smile and said, "But she'd be good for you. You should get her number."

Mom laughed as I rubbed the pain out of my leg and tried to think of something to say.

"Uncle Jason," Bethany continued calmly, as if she hadn't just assaulted me, "my mom says you keep getting dumped because you always pick the wrong girls!"

Mom laughed again. She was enjoying this a little too much. The three of us were a messed-up and broken family, but hey, at least we were family.

Once our meals arrived, I started shoveling forkfuls of enchilada into my mouth. About three bites before I could finish, another sharp kick arrived on my shin, courtesy of Bethany. Mouth full, I gave her my patented mad-dog look. She just grinned and bobbed her head to the left.

"Can I get you another beer?"

She was back again. I wondered why the most beautiful woman I'd ever seen kept torturing me, why she was laughing along with Bethany and Mom, and why my mouth was still so full of enchilada. *Think, think, think. Got it!*

"Wmmumph, wait," I asked Kristie, managing to swallow, "you're not trying to get me drunk, are you?" I was pretty proud of that line, until Kristie beamed back, and the pride in my chest got mixed up with a bunch of butterflies in my stomach.

"Actually, no," she sassed, still grinning. "Just trying to get a better tip! I'll be back in a sec with your bill."

I clamped my jaw shut to keep from sighing like a teenager saying goodbye to his fling at summer camp. I knew one thing: I couldn't leave without her number. I wiped my suddenly sweating hands on my shorts.

"Hey, Mom," I suggested, "why don't you wait outside with Bethany while I pay the bill."

Mom laughed and stood to leave. Bethany punched me on the shoulder as she walked by and whispered, "Don't mess this up, Uncle Jason!"

Normally scoring a phone number was a cinch. But this was the furthest thing from normal I'd experienced in what felt like forever. Waiting for Kristie to return with the bill, I experienced a revelation: I *needed* this woman's number. Not in some testosterone-driven way or because she was so amazingly cute. I was feeling something deeper. I was hearing something good from inside my heart. Whatever happened next, Bethany was right. I couldn't mess this up.

In the thirty seconds before Kristie returned, I came up with a brilliant plan. When she slid the bill toward me, I pulled out my wallet. Left it open for a while, so she'd notice my wallet badge.

"So, I'm kinda new in town and don't know many people . . ." I began. In that moment where I had to breathe, I suddenly regretted my plan. *New in town, seriously?* But I had to soldier on, so I continued. "So I was wondering if you wanted to catch a movie with me sometime or—"

Sometime or *what?* Things were going from bad to worse.

"You a cop?" she asked.

"Fireman. OFD," I answered. Maybe things were getting back on track. Except in response she gave the smallest of shrugs, which basically said, *Fireman? Meh.*

Damn if that didn't make her even more perfect to me. The last time I went out with a woman who didn't know I was a fireman was never. Without another word, she spun and walked to the till to grab my change.

Sautel, you screwed up! She thinks you're an arrogant jerk now!

All too soon she returned and set the bill tray down. "I never do this, but . . ."

My heart kicked up a notch.

"I'll take you up on that offer."

I looked down. On top of the receipt was a phone number written in looping digits, and beneath it, "Kristie" in cursive. Even her handwriting was perfect.

"I liked the way you were treating your mom and daughter tonight," she said.

"She's not my daughter," I laughed. "She's my niece!"

She smiled at me.

Sautel, do whatever you have to do to see that smile again. Just start talking.

"So I—"

But she was back to work already. I stayed where I was, trying to calculate the tip. It felt more complicated than decoding a lunar orbit. Too little and I'd look like a cheapskate. Too much would make me look desperate. And a normal tip would make it seem like I hadn't spent enough time trying to calculate the tip! At least all the calculating gave me a chance to take in a little more of Kristie. The way she genuinely smiled at the people she was serving. The way she squatted down when taking a child's order and nodded her head as she wrote the child's request. Everything about her showed she wasn't just working but was taking care of people. I could tell her beauty was shining for everyone in the room, not just me.

I wanted to stay there and watch her all night. But I also had enough remaining sense to know that it would make me look like a creepy perv. So at last I stood, grabbed her phone number, and walked outside.

Bethany and I said goodbye to my mom. Then when we got home we played a couple of games before bedtime. Bethany was nice enough not to mention Kristie. She could tell I was, as the saying went, in *deep smit*.

When I went to bed, I lay on my back and smiled at the ceiling. I hadn't felt this good in so long that most of me wondered if I was kidding myself. I waited for the black hole to show up. To start sucking down the happiness racing through every part of my body. Instead, I fell right asleep and didn't wake until the next morning.

With sun glowing around the corners of my window blinds, I sat up, swung my legs to the floor, and stretched my arms.

Huh. I hadn't slept so well since . . . maybe ever.

Not a single bad memory could penetrate what I was feeling. I stood, took a few deep breaths, and then laughed out loud. Because I knew the name of the thing that was filling up my chest.

This broken fireman was feeling joy.

CHAPTER 14
RESCUE

THE FIRE CALL CAME in just before midnight. From the location given by dispatch, I knew we'd be the second company due on scene.

"Can of corn, right, Seed?" Jimmy asked.

I rolled out of bed and hit the floor. "Yep, no big deal," I answered, "unless you screw something up."

He grinned and punched my shoulder as we headed to the apparatus bay to gear up.

The fire was big enough that I could see where we were headed as soon as we pulled out of the firehouse. Half a mile or so east I saw a thick column of smoke. The Oakland sky was almost always lit at night. Between the sodium-vapor lights in the harbor and the half-a-million residents living their lives, the marine layer tended to glow a soft yellow. But fire made its own mark. The smoke was boiling up and blacking out the lighter clouds, and it was lit from beneath with a wicked orange glow.

"Looks like it's rolling!" shouted Jimmy.

"Sure does!" I responded.

We knew the guys from the next station over would already be on scene because the fire was in their district. They were a double-house, so they were staffed with a four-man engine like ours and a five-man ladder truck. Since it was their fire, we'd be running backup. Once their crew breached the front door, they'd move through the interior as quickly as the conditions allowed, and we'd move in immediately behind to knock down any hot spots and search for survivors or victims the initial attack missed. Meanwhile, the ladder truck guys would be on the roof cutting ventilation holes.

We rolled up right on the tailpipes of the first engine, and me, Cappy, and Jimmy jumped down while Rog found a hydrant.

"I'll catch up with you two in a minute," Cappy told us before jogging over to have a quick face-to-face with the other captain.

We were almost to the porch when something caught my eye. This Victorian, like many, had a side driveway that led to a detached rear garage. This driveway, also like many, held a few old cars and an assortment of junk like old tires, radiators, and other rusted car parts. In the dark that stuff could bang your shin or knee something fierce. But what got my attention was an absolute geyser of smoke shooting out a first-story window and venting into the driveway. I took a few steps toward that side of the house for a better view because I thought I saw something hanging out from beneath the smoke.

Dammit! It was a human hand sticking out the window, just below the smoke line. And it was waving frantically.

I took stock of our personnel. Rog was out front, assisting the engineer from the other station drag a hose back to a fire hydrant. Cappy, as the most senior captain on scene, had taken command of the fire and was in the front yard coordinating the scene and ensuring everyone's safety.

"Cappy!" I cupped my hands and yelled. "We got a rescue in a window down the driveway!"

"Go," he yelled, "and take Jimmy, but make it fast. They haven't put any water on the fire yet!"

Two firefighters were already at the window. They'd noticed the same thing I had. On the fireground, preservation of life is always our highest priority. Me and Jimmy scrambled up the driveway to join them. A massive old Caddy sat rusting on blocks directly below the smoking window. I clambered up the front bumper and onto the hood, joining one of the other firefighters who was trying to look through the window.

"We're here," I yelled toward the hand. "Stand up and jump out!" The second I yelled, the soot-stained hand disappeared back into the smoke.

I looked over at the other firefighter. It was Marcus, a guy I knew pretty well. He knew what we had to do even before I yelled, "Let's go!"

We both strapped on our masks, activated the airflow, and climbed onto the roof of the Caddy. The heat and smoke flooding through the window were intense. Before fire enters a room, it pushes a front of superheated smoke ahead of it, like Godzilla wading through a harbor. The effect was like sitting in front of a box fan that was perched in front of an open oven.

That meant whoever the hand belonged to was inside the oven. I grabbed the windowsill, tucked my head in through the window, and pulled myself into the room with one quick motion. I knew the floor beneath the window would be quite a bit cooler . . . except I only fell eighteen inches before bouncing on top of an empty mattress.

I tried to figure out what was what in the sudden darkness. With a combination of touch and severely limited vision, I discovered I was on a hospital bed. Whoever had been waving was gone, which in this case probably meant the person was on the floor. Marcus came in behind me and bounced on the bed as well. I shoved my gloved hand right in front of his face mask and pointed down, twice. The two of us rolled off the bed and hit the floor—*thump, thump*—but the floor turned out to be a semiconscious woman lying on her side.

She was maybe four hundred pounds. Everything clicked. She was bedridden, and her family had pushed her hospital bed up against the window to give her some fresh air. When the fire hit, no one had been able to reach her room. It wasn't technically on fire yet, but for all practical purposes it was.

Our awkward arrival must have given the woman a jolt of adrenaline. Her eyes snapped wide and she screamed, "I'm burning, I'm burning, ohmygodohmygod, I'm *burning!*"

She wasn't wrong. I could feel my ears and the back of my neck crisping. It wouldn't be long before the woman died in this heat, probably before the fire even arrived.

In conditions like these we always worked by touch and sound. Flashlights were for when the fire was already out. But even our sense of touch was limited by the bulky fireproof gloves we wore. From the amount of heat pouring into the room, along with the crackling sound of the flames working their way toward us, I knew the door was open. And since the window we'd just climbed through was also open, we were in a literal chimney. Every bit of heat and smoke ahead of the fire was being sucked into that room and then out the single window.

First things first. We needed to cut off the oxygen flow and lower the temperature. I hit Marcus on the shoulder and yelled that I was going to find the door and close it. He stayed with the woman, blanketing her upper torso with his body to shield her from the rapidly increasing heat. I crawled on my belly like a soldier under razor wire toward the heat source, blindly sweeping my arms in front of me as I tried to feel for the door. Shutting it would force the superheated smoke to find another outlet. It wouldn't stop the fire, of course, but it might buy us enough time to figure out what to do next.

My shoulder hit an object that toppled forward. I slithered another little bit. My opposite knee whacked a box of some kind. I waved both arms in a 180 arc looking for the door, and all they touched was debris. Junk. *Dammit. A hoarder's house.* It was every fireman's nightmare. I knew the door wouldn't shut with all the stuff piled around the room. Worse, the fire coming toward us would be extra angry because of all the additional fuel.

I returned to the woman and tapped Marcus on the shoulder to let him know I was back. I shouted in slow, controlled sentences so he could hear me. Talking through a face mask in zero visibility and high heat limits your vocal abilities, so I had to keep it clear and concise.

What I wanted to say was, "We are absolutely screwed!"—but in words that would give him a clear picture of how bad the situation was *and* hopefully not panic the woman. I told him, "Door's blocked! Can't close! Going to window! Hold tight!"

I could hear the woman coughing and struggling to breathe. As I knelt, placed two hands on top of the mattress, and pushed my head toward the window, I thought I heard someone yelling from outside.

"Get outta there! I said get outta there, *now!*" It was Cappy. "It's gonna flashover any second!"

He was right. The room had to be seconds away from a flashover, which meant the air was on the verge of spontaneously igniting. It was suicidally hot in the room, even though nothing was actually burning yet. But at any moment it would *all* be burning. So, yeah, evacuating the room would be ideal.

There was one problem. Well, two problems: a bad one and a worse one.

Bad was that, with the open window still sucking hard on the interior of the house, the smoke pouring out of it was starting to flame. I'd felt the difference when I lifted my head to hear Cappy. If we carried the unprotected woman out that window, her entire body would be scorched. Worse was that lifting a woman her size from the floor to the window would be an impossible feat with only two firemen.

I had a brain wave. Not a good one, obviously, since it would require me to stick my head back up into the intense heat as I yelled my idea out the window. But I was out of moves and refused to leave that lady to die.

"Cappy!" I yelled, getting close enough to the window that he'd hear me. "Throw me! A bottle!"

Five seconds later a bottle and mask landed on the hospital bed. Followed by a very clear order: "Evacuate *now*!"

I ignored him. Marcus probably heard Cappy's voice too, but he wasn't going anywhere either. We really didn't have a choice. The woman was alive. We were healthy. Our job was to save her. And if we couldn't, it was going to end badly for all three of us. Saving ourselves wasn't what we'd come for.

My brain wave came from some basic facts. If the woman stayed in the room unprotected any longer, she would die. Even if we shielded most of her body, her lungs would fry. On the other hand, if we suddenly gained the strength of elephants and lifted her to the bed and then out the window, she would also die. Her lungs would still fry, *and* she'd be covered in third-degree burns.

I grabbed the SCBA bottle and mask and hit the floor again. I tapped Marcus on the shoulder and motioned for him to shift to the woman's lower body. I leaned over her torso, lifted her head, and slipped the mask over her face. And—*fwup-hisssss*—her face was sealed, and she was now breathing the same fresh air we were.

But then what? The wild card was the heat in the room. The fire was pushing it toward us like a runaway train, and it didn't show any signs of stopping.

I could sense the blisters growing bigger on my ears and neck. It was the type of heat that makes people jump out of high-rises rather than endure the scorching a second longer. Under normal firefighting conditions, that kind of heat meant you either started hitting the fire with your hose line or you got outta there. But this was far from normal firefighting conditions. With my free hand, I grabbed Marcus's shoulder and held on. We stayed as low as we could, protecting her body as best we could by taking the inferno on our backs.

I'd been on the nozzle for fires like this and knew how tough they can be to knock down. But I also knew the guys were pushing as hard as they could through the mounds of flammable garbage. Marcus knew the same thing. We just had to try and hang on and wait for our brothers to come through for us.

I twisted my neck and squinted up. Cappy had been right about the flashover. The ceiling above us was turning orange, and the heat was becoming unbearable. I yelled out to the lady, "We're here! With you!" I wanted her to know she wasn't alone, because as bad as it was, I knew we were just seconds away from it getting infinitely worse. I gritted my teeth.

Spontaneous ignition in three, two, one . . . *Boom!*

The room went absolute dark as the sweet, sweet sound of fire exploding into steam hit my blistering ears. The other station's hose line was in the hallway and darkening down the fire. The heroes behind that hose line knew they were our only hope, and they knew how hot this hoarder's fire was burning. They courageously pushed all the way into our room and hit it with a ton of water.

Then, in the relative silence, came the voice of the nozzle guy. "Hey! You clowns still alive?"

"Ya!" I yelled.

Then I realized the woman beneath me was no longer screaming, which meant she might be dead. I pulled my flashlight and aimed it at her face. Her pupils contracted, she blinked, and then her eyes closed tight. Still alive. A laugh grew in my chest. *This tough lady would make a hell of a firefighter!* I bit back the laugh, though. I was just happy she'd made it.

Within thirty seconds, our little hell had become a completely different world. The heat was gone, the fire was out, and a few other firefighters arrived to help us drag the woman through the tunnels of burned junk toward the front door.

Finally I yanked my mask off and gulped in the sweet night air. My ears and neck felt like someone was holding a flame to them. Then I grinned. *Good thing you didn't die, Sautel. Your first date with Kristie is tomorrow!*

Before heading back inside the house to finish the job, I walked to the ambulance and found one of the paramedics. "How was she?"

"Airway is fine," he answered, "and not a single serious burn."

I laughed. Of all the ideas in the world, mine were usually the most thickheaded. But it had worked.

"She was pretty pissed at whoever dragged her out so roughly, though."

I pulled a face.

"Yeah. Said whoever those guys were hurt her shoulder."

I massaged my own shoulder and winced. "Her shoulder, huh? Good thing her priorities are straight. Protecting your shoulder is *numero uno* when you're burning to death."

He chuckled and then handed me a bottle of water. "Here, pour this over your neck and ears. They're blistering up pretty bad."

"Thanks, but I'm good," I said, taking the bottle and swigging the water instead. I nodded toward the battalion chief who had arrived on scene. The paramedic followed my eyes. If the battalion chief caught on to how bad I was blistered up, he'd force me to fill out an injury report. I took another swig of water and handed the bottle back, saying to the paramedic, "Plus, I *hate* paperwork."

He nodded and chuckled again. We bumped fists.

Then I turned and walked back into the burned-out skeleton of the house, still grinning about my date with Kristie.

CHAPTER 15

FIRST DATE

OUR ENGINE HAD REACHED the burning Victorian just after midnight, and the last visible flame was doused only ten minutes later. Hauling and sorting the unending piles of junk *after* the fire, though? Pretty much the penthouse in downtown suck-city.

When I'd entered the house again after checking with the paramedic, I went to the attic first to pull down what was left of the ceiling and roof. Marcus, the firefighter from the other station who'd been in the room with me, was there as well, and two of his guys were giving him grief for making a rescue with a guy from Station 11. I walked up behind him and acted like I was going to slap his blistered neck.

"Do it and die, Seed!" he warned.

Then we all laughed, bumped fists, and got to work.

It was the same procedure for every structure fire: go through the remains of the building, drag out any solid objects, and make sure they weren't still smoldering. There's a whole lot of combustible material in the aftermath of most fires, and all it takes is one secret hot spot to reignite the whole shebang a few hours later. On a normal fire, the job is manageable. It takes ninety minutes or so to pull out a couch and a couple mattresses, cut out the carpet, and strip all the sheetrock off the walls and ceiling to look for hidden fire. This is when any new guys get to play firefighter as they hit each piece with a fan of water, then break it up with an ax or a boot to make sure the fire is all the way dead.

This house was the worst I'd ever seen for hoarding. By the time we'd lugged everything outside, it seemed like the pile in the front yard was bigger than the house itself. Usually the pile out front could fit in a large pickup truck or two. This house needed three industrial dump trucks to haul it all away to the city dump.

We didn't make it back to the firehouse until four in the morning. Then we still had to wash down and clean our equipment and get everything ready for the next run—at which point Cappy hauled me into his office and demanded a blow-by-blow of what had happened from my perspective. I guessed he was pissed about me and Marcus disobeying a direct order. Marcus's captain was probably doing the same thing at the other station.

I was too tired to care. And I'd done what I had to do. I'd make exactly the same choice the next time. We had to fight fire like humans, not robots.

Finally, I grabbed a quick shower and flopped onto my bed. And I still felt . . . happy.

First date with Kristie in thirteen hours.

I grinned and fell dead asleep. It was nearly dawn.

I woke to the sound of someone knocking on the dorm room door.

I looked at my nightstand clock: 8:10 a.m. *Wake up, Sautel!* Jimmy and Rog were already up and in the kitchen.

I was always up by 6:30 a.m., waiting in the kitchen to chat it up with the first guy coming through on duty. And if it was a new kid, waiting to yell something like, "That mop ain't gonna push itself, rookie!" We'd all paid our dues, and most of us survived.

"Seed, you up yet?" Captains ran the firehouse, but they also followed tradition, which clearly stated that captains were not allowed in dorm rooms unless invited. Mostly it kept them from having to do extra paperwork by walking in on us doing something against city regs.

I rubbed the sleep out of my eyes and said, yawning, "Yeah, come in."

Cappy stepped into the room. "Last night, when I wanted to hear your version of what happened for my report, it wasn't because you were in trouble. Anyways, I just wanted to say, good job, kid. I recommended you guys for a commendation."

That didn't sound right, and in my still-hazy state I just stared at him. What in the world would we be getting commended for? Moving the most burned junk ever from inside to outside?

Cappy chuckled. "Sautel, you look even dumber than normal right now."

No way to argue that one. I just shrugged.

"It was your bright idea to use the bottle on that lady, right?"

I nodded, then stood up and stretched. *Oof.* My back was *not* in good shape. Maybe that lady had been closer to five hundred pounds.

"Turns out no one's ever thought to use our gear on a civilian before. And somehow . . . somehow *your* thick head came up with that brilliant idea first!"

I frowned. "A commendation for *that*?" I waved my hand dismissively. "Tell the brass to keep it. My reward comes in the form of my paycheck every two weeks."

"Yeah, well, you're up for one, along with Marcus from the other station, plus the other two guys who were on the nozzle that saved your asses. Like it or not, you're gonna have to dress up real nice and go play kiss-ass downtown."

I knew it would take six months to a year for anything official to happen. If they actually did hold an awards assembly for us, chances were I'd have something important going on that would prevent me from showing up. Rearranging my sock drawer, say.

Cappy laughed at my sour expression. His laughs were often right on the border between *at* and *with*. "Anyways," he continued, "last night at dinner you mentioned you had a date tonight, right?"

Rubbing my belly, I asked, "Did we even *have* dinner last night?"

He laughed again. "Yeah, that fire took it out of me too."

Cappy was a working man's officer through and through. We'd found literal buckets of feces in a couple of rooms in that house, and he had been right there with us, shoulder to shoulder, until the cleanup was finished. "Seed, the reason I'm bringing up your date is because I saw your eyes light up, right before you punched Jimmy for taking bets on how long it would take her to walk out on you."

Uh-oh. We were *real* close to father-son chat territory. Still, I'd listen to whatever Cappy said. He'd earned it.

"From what you've said, this girl sounds like a good one, Jason. Just be yourself. The Jason *I* know is the one this girl deserves."

Before the silence got awkward, he turned to leave. Then, just as the door was getting ready to close, he stuck his head back in and said, "Oh, and the battalion chief wanted me to tell you that if you ever disobey a direct order again, I have the green light to put my boot up your ass."

The door closed, but I could still hear him laughing as he walked across the apparatus bay floor.

I hopped out of my bunk, then grabbed my bedding and folded it into my locker. Normally I'd go over and have a laugh with the oncoming crew, but not today. I just wanted to head home and get ready.

Date with Kristie, Sautel. Somehow you got a date with Kristie.

—◇—

The two weeks since I'd managed to get Kristie's number at La Cantina had been a blur.

Bethany had packed my days off with movies, hikes, restaurants, and board games, and when I went to work, she'd hung out with my mom. The whole time I hadn't been able to stop thinking about Kristie. A small part of that was due to Bethany's nonstop teasing, but the bigger reason was that I'd fallen in deep. Every morning when my eyes opened, Kristie popped into my head, and she was the last thing I thought of before going to sleep.

And I was actually *sleeping*, not just nightmaring with my eyes closed.

We'd only been able to connect on the phone twice, but I'd learned a few important details. One, she lived with her brother and his wife and kids. Two, she loved spending time with her grandparents. That was obvious from the moment I heard an elderly voice in the background scolding her to hang up on "that fireman" and get back to her studies. Three, she was a full-time nursing student at Sonoma State. And four, she also worked full time at La Cantina. She either had a time machine or didn't sleep.

The weirdest part of the two-week wait was that I hadn't wanted our date to come any sooner. I mean, I'd *wanted* it to, but I was okay with the wait because I had Bethany. Being a functional uncle had felt good, like my relationship with my niece had lifted me onto a rock from out of the muck and misery I usually floundered in. Over the years, my survival skills—survive school, survive my parents' divorce, survive dark and suicidal thoughts, survive a life of fighting fire—had become deeply ingrained habits, and truly caring about someone else just didn't fit the pattern. Bethany had started to change that. In small ways when I flew to visit her, yeah, but big-time when she came to visit me.

I'd dropped Bethany at the airport the day before the hoarder fire. When the flight attendant met us at the gate, I said, "Take care of my precious cargo, please." Then I gave Bethany a bear hug and a kiss on top of her head. I quickly turned around, because I didn't want either of them to notice I'd started crying. After a couple of steps, I couldn't resist turning back to catch one last glimpse of my niece.

She was already walking down the jetway when I called to her. "I'll see you soon, I promise!"

She was crying too. We both tried to smile and we both failed.

I waited the whole rest of that day for my black hole to start eating away at the happiness Bethany had brought into my life. It never happened. What I felt was no longer depression or evil or self-loathing or anxiety while awaiting the next episode of darkness to come along.

I felt like crap, yeah. But I could still smile through the tears, because for the first time in a long while, the only thing I was feeling was good old-fashioned sadness.

There. I tossed the last cleaning rag in the washing machine and closed the lid. My house was officially spick-and-span . . . and my back was on *fire*.

The fire was also spreading down the back of both legs, so I called my doc to see if he could sneak me in. The only appointment would conflict with my date, so I politely hung up and tossed down four more Advil. And then, with no other way to pass the hours until Kristie arrived, I did something unusual: I took a relaxed, content nap. My body had taken a pretty good beating the night before, but for once my mind and heart felt like they could recuperate.

At 4:30 p.m., my alarm woke me in time to get ready for Kristie's arrival at 7:00 p.m. for our dinner reservation. The house was already perfect. And it would take me only about ten minutes to shower and dress. *Why didn't I set my alarm for 6:45 p.m.?* I had roughly infinity minutes to obsess about Kristie and pace in circles.

Kristie had asked me to decide where we'd eat. Normally on dates I'd pick loud places so I could avoid giving away too much of myself. Tonight, though, was a whole different ball game. I chose a quaint Italian place downtown called Giuseppe's Grotto that advertised itself as *très chic*, which I assumed was French for a good place to take chicks.

Kristie wasn't like anyone I'd ever met. I mean, even *I* wasn't like myself anymore. I couldn't get my mind off Kristie or forget the moment I had first seen her beauty radiating across the room. I was desperate to be near her, to listen to her, to connect with her. I wanted to know all about her interests, her past, her dreams.

To pass the time, I talked myself through the date. *Okay, Sautel, calm down. You can do this. All you have to do is think of a good opening line, then guess how she'll answer. And then, based on what you think she'll answer, you can come up with a few ways to take the conversation. Then later you can always circle back to the options you didn't use, depending on—*

At last it was close enough to 7:00 p.m. that I could get ready. First came my third shower of the day, followed by a nice shave. Kristie seemed like the kind of woman who would appreciate a smooth cheek. Then a tiny bit of cologne. And, finally, my ultimate date outfit. The only way I knew to dress nicely for a date was to compare it to how I *normally* dressed. My number of typical outfit styles was three: fire gear when on call, and T-shirt and shorts at all other times, except when I wriggled into my wetsuit for surfing.

I checked myself in the mirror for the tenth time. The one button-up shirt I owned looked fine. The one pair of pants I owned— Levi's 501s—looked maybe better than fine. I turned sideways in the mirror. Was Kristie a leg girl? Maybe I should tuck my shirt in and show off what my mama gave me. Or maybe she was more of a chest girl, and I should go down a button or two . . .

Ding-dong. Doorbell meant go time.

The feeling reminded me of pulling up to my first large fire. My first thought had been, *This could be my final day on earth.* But my second, adrenaline-powered thought had been, *Let's do this!*

I pulled myself together and casually strolled across my living room. Then I opened the door. *Holyyy shhh . . . cow,* I corrected myself. *Hide the potty mouth in front of Kristie.* But my goodness was she the medicine I needed! She was wearing a cute knee-high skirt with pink flowers on it, a pink top, and a thin, white button-up sweater over the pink top that matched her white sandals. Her blond hair was pulled back in a high ponytail.

When I leaned against the doorframe, cool as can be, I almost fell over. I quickly recovered and gave her a polite hug, then invited her in.

She stood in the entryway with her hands on her hips. "Wow, nice place!" She nodded approvingly. "How long have you lived here?"

"A little over two years. I—"

Her laugh interrupted me. I laughed a little, then stopped. *Wait, what are we laughing about?*

"So," she continued, smiling right at me, "do you *always* lie to girls?"

Uh-oh. That sounded bad. But she was looking seriously good. The whole thinking thing was starting to get more difficult. *Quick, Sautel.* I recovered, asking a brilliant counter question, "What?"

"When you asked for my phone number, you told me you were new in town." She took one hand from her hip and gestured around the house. "But now you're telling me you've lived here for two years."

This was not good.

"So . . . which is it?"

"I, um," I started. "It's just that, well . . ."

She interrupted me with another laugh. I could have listened to that laugh all night long. Not that I wanted to get grilled about lying all night long. But still.

"Got you!" she announced. "Remember, I do have a good memory, so *you* better be careful."

"Hey, I had to come up with something quick," I said, trusting the good humor I saw in her face, "and that's all I had!" *Okay, she's still smiling.* I decided to try and wrap things up. "But at least it got you here, and you haven't left yet, so let's go eat!"

"Great!" she responded, spinning around and heading toward the door. "I'll drive."

Did she know her skirt flew up when she spun around? I followed her outside and pulled up short. Her car was about the size of Barbie's. While I wasn't a giant, I was partial to not kissing my knees while riding.

"Kristie?"

She looked back.

"Grown men my size don't ride in girly convertibles. We'll take my truck."

She laughed again. Maybe this was going to turn out okay.

I'd never even been inside Giuseppe's Grotto. I earned a pretty good paycheck and spent almost nothing, so I could have eaten there three times a week. But since I was just as happy with a burrito or a slice of take-out pizza, I didn't bother.

As we waited to be seated, I leaned toward Kristie and stage-whispered, "I never wear pants, so . . ."

She gave my legs a once over. "Well," she laughed. "Thanks for not taking me on a date in your boxers!"

I had the next part all figured out. A fancy date meant wine. So, after we were seated and our server arrived, I asked if he could bring us a bottle. Kristie smiled again. *Nice, Sautel.*

"Of course, sir. Red or white?"

Uh oh, Sautel, you didn't quite have it figured out, did you?

"Umm," I started, looking at Kristie, "I think . . ."

"Red," she said. *Boom. That's what I was about to say.*

"And did sir have a preference on the type?"

"Red," I said. "Didn't you hear the lady?"

When our server returned, he poured a tiny bit into a glass and handed the glass to me. I looked at him, and he looked at me. I took a sip and he kept looking at me, but this time with one eyebrow raised.

I got the message and took another sip, then declared, "Yep, tastes like wine to me!"

Kristie burst out laughing, followed by our waiter, followed by me. *You're crushing it, Sautel.*

The moment our server left, Kristie started talking and never stopped. And I loved every single second of it. All I wanted to do was absorb all the goodness and joy that was pouring out of her as we sat together. It seemed like hours later when the check arrived, and Kristie quickly offered to pay.

"Sure," I said, grabbing the bill, "you could try to do that. But two things. One, you'd have to walk back to *your* car that's parked at my place in those floppy sandals. And two," pointing to myself, "you wouldn't get to go on a second date with *this* guy."

She laughed. "Fine, fine. You pay! I'm a starving student and can't afford to eat here anyway."

I started to laugh back, then bit my lip.

"I mean, that's why I work where I work," she said, looking down. "At La Cantina." She blushed like she'd just done something wrong.

I frowned. "What are—"

"I work there so I can eat. I'm a true starving student, not just one who pretends to be."

She'd shared with me something I'd never experienced on a first date, or maybe on any date: honesty.

Eventually I answered, "I get it. I'm a high school dropout. If it weren't for my mom pushing me to take the high school proficiency test, I wouldn't be where I am now. There was a time in my life when adding Spam to my ramen was a special treat."

She looked back up. "Jason," she said, her face extremely serious, "I've *never* been hungry enough to eat Spam!"

We both laughed hard enough to turn every head in Giuseppe's.

The laughter made me willing to open up about my past. As we continued to sit, finishing off the wine, I shared about my rough childhood and how the memories still devastated me.

"Jason," Kristie asked kindly, "your whole childhood wasn't unhappy, was it? What about the good times?"

My glass froze halfway to my mouth, and then I set it down. It was maybe the first time I'd considered the question, at least without immediately being overwhelmed by the stench of my cruelest, darkest memories. My dad had suffered his way through a hard life, and he'd taken me along for the ride on that pain train. But Kristie was right. Objectively, my *whole* childhood hadn't been a horror show.

To my surprise I found myself chuckling as I told a story about my dad. "This one time me and Dad took a road trip in his VW Rabbit all the way to Oregon. In the middle of some forest I saw a deer bounding toward the car and I screamed, which made Dad scream. And then the deer absolutely *smacked* off Dad's door. Screwed it up good! So, for the rest of the trip, he had to use my door to get in and out."

Kristie raised an eyebrow. "*That's* your happy story?"

"I mean, it was happy for *us*," I answered. Then I told her how Dad had helped me get through paramedic school by letting me move back in with him, and how he'd beamed with pride when I graduated from the academy. I admitted I'd lashed out at him and been ungrateful and difficult.

"But don't we all do that?" she asked.

"Do what?"

"Let our bad stories push the good ones aside," she answered, "especially when we're struggling with something hard. But do yourself a favor, Jason, and try to make good stories your priority."

I had never been to a therapist before, but that little piece of advice hit me right where I needed it. I tried my best not to stare at her in awe. She'd given me something I totally needed, and she did it kindly.

Later we stepped onto the sidewalk outside the restaurant. Kristie took my hand and said, "Now let's go for a walk."

Yep. Anything to make this night last longer.

Downtown Santa Rosa had a certain charm: art deco buildings, old houses transformed into flower shops and cafés, and countless clothing and jewelry stores. The trees lining the streets had decorative white lights on them year-round.

Kristie led me from window to window, pointing out the art and outfits she liked. "Window shopping is one of my favorite things to do," she said.

"Window shopping?"

She pointed at the display of colored candles we were standing in front of and repeated, "Window shopping."

"Okay, I've honestly never heard of that. But yeah, I love window shopping too."

"It's not forever," she said, a few storefronts later. "Once I become a nurse and make some money, maybe I'll make *shopping* a pastime and leave out the window part."

"I dunno," I said. "Shopping means you'd be going inside the smelly candle store."

She turned to look up at me.

I squeezed her hand and told her, "I don't love smelly candle stores, but I could get used to staying outside with you."

—◇—

Back at my house, I held open the door of her convertible as she climbed in. Then, with the car door still open, I squatted down so we could be at eye level.

Mistake. Now I knew what it felt like to be stabbed in the back with forty dinner forks at once. My face must have given it away.

"You poor thing, go rest your back."

I nodded.

"And on our next date, I want to hear about that fire."

I grinned. *Next date.* "It's a deal."

Except I didn't move. Just gritted my teeth behind my lips and gave a small smile. *You've dealt with pain before, Sautel. You can still look hot. You got this. It'll be worth it when you steal a kiss from your green-eyed wonder. Sure, you wouldn't ride in a convertible this tiny if you were escaping the zombie apocalypse. But just look at Kristie sitting there in her skirt, hotter than . . .*

I mentally slapped myself back to reality. Unfortunately, Kristie continued to face forward. She didn't seem to be picking up what I was putting down. It was time to move things along before my back completely seized and I fell backward onto the asphalt. Bracing one hand on her door, I leaned in toward her. I closed my eyes and tried to relax my back. I was about to taste those tender lips for the first time and . . . *Blech!*

I jerked my head back and opened my eyes to see a tiny, smiling clown face. I'd just kissed an antenna ball.

"Isn't he cute?" Kristie asked. "I got him the other week from Jack in the Box, and I keep him in the car with me."

Now it felt like someone had replaced the forks in my back with superheated fireplace pokers. "He's cute, I guess," I managed to answer, "but he's not a great kisser."

She laughed.

I pouted.

She turned toward me. *Finally!* She put both of her hands on my face and slowly turned my head. Then she graced my right cheek with the sweetest, softest, most amazing kiss in the history of the world.

It had to be. There was no way it wasn't.

"Good night, Jason."

Then, still holding my face, she gently pushed me backward. I managed to stand and step back without screaming in pain. She closed her door, started her car, and, looking at me from behind her window, gave me one last smile before pulling away from the curb.

I stood there in the dark, mesmerized. I stared until her taillights disappeared.

What was happening to me?

CHAPTER 16

HIT AND RUNNING

MY CELL PHONE RANG me awake. By the time I untangled myself from the sheet, rolled over, and fumbled around on top of my nightstand, the call had gone to voice mail. I sat up and tried to focus on the blurry red numbers of my alarm clock: 6:45 a.m.

It had to be the station calling to see if I wanted some overtime. I ignored my phone and shuffled to the bathroom. While I did my business, I heard the voice mail ping back in the bedroom. Normally I would work as much overtime as possible. Not for the money, but because when I went to work I got to help people, and helping people kept my mind off my own misery. Today, though, I just felt like hanging out and getting some stuff done around the house—and, of course, thinking about Kristie the whole time.

I walked back into my bedroom and picked up the phone. Suddenly I was almost laughing out loud. It wasn't the station. It was Kristie. Without bothering to listen to her message, I punched the callback button.

I could tell right away she was out jogging. "Hey," she said, breathing hard, "you awake?"

"I am now!"

"I was just calling to check on your back. How is it?"

"Well," I hedged, "it *was* feeling better, but now it's hurting again. You know, since I was jarred awake by an early morning phone call."

Kristie laughed. "Ha! I thought you were supposed to be a big, tough fireman?"

"Only when I'm working," I responded. "The rest of the time I'm kind of a wimp."

Another laugh. *That's a good sign.* "Well, I'm glad you're feeling better," she said. "But now I have to finish my morning workout and get to school. Have a great day."

Then silence. She'd hung up on me! I wasn't exactly a ladies' man, but even I knew that was a bad sign. Or was it? She'd been laughing. And she'd been the one to call me, not the other way around. Still, there was no denying I'd been hung up on. I fell back onto my pillow and stared at the ceiling. I was blown away. That pretty much never happened to me. Not the hanging-up part, which I'd unfortunately experienced, but the part where someone cared enough about me to check in and see how I was doing. That was a bit much for my brain to process that early in the morning, never mind my heart.

Maybe if I stare at the ceiling some more I can figure things out. Maybe I should . . . call her back.

Given my dark, lonely, and even suicidal childhood, I was all too familiar with direct voices in my head. Thing is, they were never this positive. Typically I had to force myself to ignore those dark voices, but this time, instead of overthinking it, I grabbed the phone and punched redial.

When Kristie answered, I said, "Since we're throwing all the call-back dating rules out the window, now it's my turn."

"Jason," she said, "I don't follow silly rules. I follow my heart, and my heart said to call you earlier."

"Well, you just taught me something, because *my* heart told me to call you back."

Another laugh. *Yes!* This was going better than it had any right to. Her laugh sounded amazing, and I knew I'd do almost anything to hear it again. But she brought me back to reality. "Okay, you called me," she said, "but make it quick. Remember, I want to finish my workout."

Time to move forward with my ingenious plan, which I had created the instant before. "I've got a situation here," I began. "An emergency, really, and, um . . . I need your help."

"Oh really, mister tough guy," she kidded. "What's your emergency?"

"It's my coffee pot," I said. "It's broken, and I have a medical condition that requires me to have coffee before I leave the house."

There was that laugh again. Music to my ears.

"Listen, this is serious," I said, hamming it up. "I could *die*."

"And I'm supposed to believe that?"

"Well, the lie I told you about being new in town worked," I replied, "so I figured this one might work too."

After a brief hesitation, she said, "Look, I'll drop a cup of joe off for you, but I'm leaving it on the porch. I'm all sweaty from my workout, and besides, I'm late for school."

"Sure!"

"Oh," she continued, "and I'm not bothering to put any cream or sugar in it, so deal with it!"

For once I kept my mouth shut. I took my coffee black anyway, so keeping quiet was a win-win.

Ten minutes later I was dressed, my teeth were brushed, and I was standing at the front window, looking through the blinds. I watched Kristie's convertible pull up to the curb. And since she didn't know I was spying on her, I watched her lean up to check her hair in the rearview mirror and quickly apply some lipstick. Another good sign.

As she walked toward my house, I opened the front door and smiled, then stepped onto the porch.

She quickly handed me a Styrofoam cup and stood on her tiptoes to kiss me—but suddenly the angel choir I'd started to hear was cut off mid-hallelujah as she spun around, mid-peck, and walked back to her car without saying a word.

I had to stall her, so I yelled the first thing that popped into my head. "Wait, you don't stink all that bad, so you can hang out for a few!"

Smooth, Sautel. Real smooth.

Unsurprisingly, my line didn't convince Kristie to stay. Surprisingly, though, she turned and flashed me one more of her amazing smiles before calling from the curb, "Not all of us are blessed with a fireman's schedule. *I* gotta get to school."

Then she hopped in her convertible and zipped off to Sonoma State.

The day was absolutely perfect after that. Time off work. Warm California sunshine soaking into me. A cup of the best gas station coffee I'd ever had in my life. Pure blue sky. And the surf report suggested it would be a great day to paddle out and enjoy some me-time with the sharks, provided my back was up to it.

My day got even better when Kristie called later that afternoon, wanting to make plans to see me again. Since I had to work a double shift the next day, I told her I'd stop by her college and take her out to lunch on my way home two days later.

"I'll be looking forward to it," she said as she hung up.

So would I. Having something to look forward to felt like it was changing everything inside me, and for whatever reason, the darkness hadn't moved in to destroy it yet.

—◇—

The following morning at the station, as I started working, I experienced the strange sensation of happiness.

At the same time, I tried to guard my emotions. I was still scared the blackness inside me was going to push Kristie away, just like it did with every other woman I'd dated. But Kristie seemed unique. She *was* unique. She cared about the way I was actually feeling. She wasn't interested in the image I presented but in the real me. That felt good—but it was also terrifying. I'd allowed her to see only bits and pieces of my true self. Most of the time I didn't even allow *me* to see my true self.

I immediately began my routine. I checked my gear, starting with the stuff that could kill me if it failed. First came my SCBA, then the fire hoses and nozzles. Last came my medical gear. Part of the reason for my routine, like any firefighter, was to be prepared for an emergency at all times. If everything was in its place and ready to go, then I'd be ready to go at a moment's notice too. But another reason was as a defense against thinking too much—or feeling too much.

I was mopping the tile floor in the kitchen when Jimmy hollered across the room, "Yo, Seed!"

I looked over at him.

He raised an eyebrow and kind of smirked at me. Then he asked what was up.

"Nothing's up," I answered. "Just cleaning."

He was still smirking.

So I stopped working and leaned on the mop and gave him a *look*.

"Well, here's the thing," he said at last. "I know something's up, because I've never, *ever* seen Jason Sautel smile while he works. Let alone whistle."

Had I been whistling? That seemed pretty unlikely. Before I could consider any further, Rog chimed in, "Can confirm. Jason's pretty much always yelling at a new kid, or if he's *really* in a good mood, he's setting up a practical joke on someone else."

That sounded more like me—but what were they getting at? Again, before I could figure anything out, Jimmy kept at it. "Hey, Cappy," he hollered from the kitchen, "you better drug test Sautel. He must have stopped by that crack house three doors down to get a little pick-me-up before his shift!"

It occurred to me that the mop I was holding would make a pretty decent weapon. Even though it was me against everyone, I had the element of surprise. But before I could decide which wise guy to take a "playful" swing at, Cappy entered the room and added his two cents.

"I know that look on Sautel's face," he said, walking into the center of the room to grab our attention. Then he pointed at me. "That boy is in *looove*."

My knuckles whitened on the mop handle. I ignored the lesser hyenas surrounding me and focused on Captain Lion. If I could take him out, the others would run. Seeing my loving attention coming his way, Cappy sprinted into the officer's quarters and locked the door behind him. I gave an incredibly polite knock with my mop handle to let him know I was still outside.

By that point everyone was laughing, including me. I had to hand it to the guys—they'd gotten me good, and I didn't have a comeback. Cappy knew exactly what he'd done. The ammunition he'd handed Rog and Jimmy would last them the rest of the shift and beyond. My revenge would have to wait until all the lovey-dovey stuff died down.

Before long it was time for chow and then family hour. The hour following lunch and dinner was a ritual for us. Unless we were interrupted by a call, we'd hang around as one big family and talk about life, work, and anything else that needed airing out. It was how we survived. It was also one of the ways we knew we could trust each other with our lives. At the dinner table, there was no rank—just family.

After that we had some free time. Since the weather was great, we decided to head behind the firehouse and get a little pickleball tournament going. We'd been going at it pretty hard for about an hour when a voice demanded our attention.

"Fireman, hurry, hurry, my little sister just got hit by a car!"

I whipped my head around and saw a neighborhood girl standing at the back gate. "Where?" I yelled. "Where's your sister?"

She pointed to her right, the direction of a busy intersection. All of us rushed inside to grab gear. Cappy called fire dispatch and told them we had a front door report of an auto versus pedestrian and to assign us to the call. Meanwhile I sprinted past the engine and reached the button to raise the apparatus door. As I punched it, I saw two older men yelling into the station that we needed to hurry.

Leaving the other crew to get the engine up and running, I ducked under the rising door and sprinted up the street, wearing only a pair of shorts, a T-shirt, and running shoes.

One hundred feet. I could see a body in the middle of the street. It wasn't moving. A crowd gathered in a semicircle around it.

Fifty feet. I could see the girl clearly, facedown on the pavement. Bystanders were screaming and crying.

Twenty-five feet. I observed the blood spreading on the street around the girl's head. "Oh my God!" I heard someone yell. "That car was going seventy! He never even slowed down!"

Ten feet. My brain detached from the surrounding scene and focused on the girl.

I slammed to a stop and hit the ground beside the girl, crouching in a pool of blood. I rolled the girl over slowly, observing what was left of the back of her head. My plan had been to get her onto her back so I could open up her airway and do whatever else I could to help her survive, if only for one minute more. But she was already gone.

Two sounds hit me at the same time. The first was the familiar wail of the fire engine as Rog rolled up to block the intersection. That would give us the space to safely work on the little girl without being hit by another speeding car. The second was the agonizing wail of a mother whose life had just been relocated from normal to the bottom of an ocean of pain. I looked up to see her sprinting down the street toward us.

In moments she was going to come face-to-face with her young daughter lying dead on the asphalt. I yelled at Jimmy to bring a yellow fire blanket. I quickly wrapped it around the little girl's head to hide the massive trauma the speeding car had inflicted. I lifted her body and sat down in the middle of the pool of blood and bone fragments, hoping to use my body to shield the mother from seeing them. Then I pulled the girl into my lap and draped the rest of the blanket as wide as I could.

The mother arrived, screaming, and dropped to the ground beside me. I told her that her sweet little daughter was gone.

I held the girl tight. I couldn't risk the blanket coming unwrapped from the back of her head. The mother held her daughter along with me, hugging and kissing the girl's face. How long we sat there was impossible to guess. We sat as long as it took.

Eventually I became aware of a police chaplain standing nearby. He sized up the situation in an instant, and I confirmed his unspoken question with a glance. Safely, slowly, respectfully, he crouched down and began to move the mother away.

With the mother's back turned, Jimmy brought two more yellow blankets and helped me stand. The first blanket was draped over the girl's body, and the second was wrapped around my gore-spattered body.

There were enough other guys on scene by then that Cappy told me to head back to the station. Rog walked back with me in silence. Once there, I dropped the yellow fire blanket to the ground and moved toward one of our exterior hoses. I stood like a statue, head down, as Rog hosed me down to get the worst of it off. As the cold water blasted me, only my fingers moved, flexing on their own. When he turned off the hose, I peeled off my shorts and T-shirt and tossed them in the dumpster.

Inside, I hit the showers. The steam had already filled the stall when Rog yelled to me, "Jason, private line!"

"Take a message!" I yelled back. I continued trying to scrub the scene from my body. And my mind.

When I finally stepped out of the shower, I checked the chalkboard beside the phone. The only thing on it was Kristie's number. I called her back.

"Jason, hi! How was your day?"

I told her what we had for lunch and how our pickleball tournament was interrupted by a call. "You know how it is," I said. "Just another day at the office."

—◇—

The morning after, I opened my eyes and the first thing I thought of was Kristie.

Two hours later, my double shift finally ended, and I hopped in my truck and gunned it to the grocery store, then to Sonoma State, where Kristie and I planned to meet for lunch. As I pulled up, I could see her waving at me from the grass across the parking lot. I parked, grabbed our turkey sandwiches and Snapples, and headed over to the picnic table she had reserved for us under a giant oak tree. She gave me a huge hug, like the kind you give someone you haven't seen in forever, then planted a kiss on my cheek and said she was happy to see me.

I sat and ate my sandwich, listening to her talk about her classes and the shift she'd put in as a waitress. Suddenly she stopped and said, "I'm sorry I'm talking so much. But I'm just happy to see you!"

Truth was, I didn't want her to stop. I didn't have anything to say. It was like all the words had been vacuumed out of my head. Plus, I loved listening to her. I could have sat there all day, soaking it in. But she lifted her sandwich and ordered me to take my turn while she ate.

"So your shift," she prompted me. "Did you have any fires?"

"No fires, but we did have a tough call." I took a swig of Snapple. "A little girl was run over and killed right down the street from our station. I arrived first and pronounced her dead. And I had to tell the girl's mom."

Kristie's sandwich dropped from her hand and hit the table, spilling open. I looked back at her face and noticed tears.

Something inside me grew heavier. Twitched. I couldn't bring myself to look her in the eyes. I'd allowed my filter to slip for a single second, and it felt like I'd thrown a wrench into the whole relationship. Could I fix what I'd done? What *had* I done? I knew I deserved whatever came next.

Kristie stood.

This is it, Sautel.

Next thing I knew she straddled the bench on my side of the picnic table, and with one arm around my left shoulder, and her head on my right shoulder, she pulled me tight.

"I don't know what to say, Jason, but I can give you a hug."

It felt like . . . everything. Like lightness.

"I'm sorry," I managed eventually. "I shouldn't have made you cry."

She sat back, then turned my head so I was looking at her. She was still weeping. "*You* didn't make me cry. What happened to you and that girl and that girl's mother is what made me cry. I'm crying for all of you."

She hugged me again. "Try not to dwell on what happened yesterday, Jason. Think about that little girl in heaven instead of in the street. Okay?"

I swallowed. Why was this woman in my life? What had I done to deserve her? I looked down.

She squeezed me so I would look up at her again. And the moment I did, she asked, "You believe in Jesus, right?"

CHAPTER 17

UNCHARTED TERRITORY

I **SO WANTED TO** tell Kristie I believed in Jesus.

Unfortunately, it was for the worst reason: to keep her in my world. I didn't believe in Jesus. Not even a little bit. But I definitely believed in dating Kristie. My life hadn't taught me anything positive about religion. Still, even I could work out that lying about Jesus to get a girl would backfire, probably in more ways than one.

Panic started to pull at my heart, my lungs, my stomach. The feeling was rare. I could count on one hand the number of times I'd panicked as an adult, and it had never been about a girl. Normally I'd crack wise and change the subject, but I couldn't with Kristie sitting right beside me on the bench of our picnic table. She deserved different. Trouble was, cracking wise was all I knew to do in a situation like that.

The weirdest part was I couldn't turn my head away. She was sitting so close I could smell her. Every ounce of habit and desire was telling me to break the stare and wait out the awkwardness, but instead, I just kept looking into her green eyes. And I felt . . . good.

Tell her the truth, Sautel. Do what you never do and let her know who you are.

As I searched for words, an image jumped into my mind: the face of the man on the Bay Bridge. He and I had locked eyes as he fell to his death, and I'd seen something, *someone*, inside him—an evil presence that had claimed him. What I was seeing in Kristie's eyes now was the undoing of all that. Hopelessness overcome by hope. Terror and fear absorbed by love. Who *was* this woman?

The only way I could finally speak was to look straight ahead. I focused on a nearby oak tree, took a long breath, and said, "Honestly, I don't know what to believe."

I felt Kristie put a hand on my back.

"Something's going on with me right now," I continued, "and—"

"Jason."

I shut up.

She moved her hand from my back to my hand, inviting me to stand. I rose and took a step back from the picnic table. She lifted her leg over the bench, stood, and wrapped her arms around me. It was like she could see how lost I was. Maybe even that she could see where I'd come from and where I was headed. She sensed I was beaten down, broken, and she was telling me I was going to be okay without using words. Normally that intimate of a moment—that emotional of a moment—would have practically killed me.

This time it felt like medicine.

It was a long time before Kristie pulled away. She looked up at me. "I'm done waitressing tonight at ten. At ten-o-five," she said, nodding for emphasis, "I'm going to find you sitting in the bookstore coffee shop across the street with a white chocolate mocha."

"But I drink black coffee!"

She frowned something fierce.

"Oh, for *you*," I said, realizing. "Okay, I'll be there."

She was still frowning. There was less than a foot of space between us. She rose on her tiptoes and tried her best to look like a tough girl—and mostly succeeded—though, to be honest, she was the hottest tough girl I'd ever laid eyes on. Then cupping her hands on either side of my face, she forced me to look right into her green, green eyes. She could have asked me to do anything at that moment, and I would have agreed.

"Jason, *promise* me you'll be there," she insisted.

"I promise! I promise!"

With that, she let go of my face and practically skipped across the grass back to her car. I shook my head and grinned. I worked beside some of the bravest people in the world, and Kristie was every bit their equal.

Whatever joy I'd been experiencing evaporated by the time I climbed into my truck and shut the door.

I was going to lose her. It was just a matter of when and how stupidly. I considered headbutting the steering wheel. *You* should *feel like this, Sautel. She's gonna be another in your long line of failures. And it's gonna be your own fault.*

I couldn't disagree. It would probably be best to ditch our coffee date. At least that way the pain would be over sooner.

The problem was, though, I couldn't imagine not seeing Kristie again. Yeah, the few weeks of knowing her provided a pretty limited amount of data. But it wasn't that long ago I was ready to take a one-way paddle into the Pacific Ocean. I'd wanted to end my life because I'd felt 100 percent hopeless—and now that wasn't true any longer. Kristie was amazing and beautiful and smart and funny, of course, but what really made me want to be with her was that I wanted to catch what she had. Her love and her goodness felt contagious. Maybe even someone like me could get infected.

But no, I decided. It would never work. I could *want* it to work, but that wouldn't take either of us off the paths we were on. She was a good person, doing good things in the world, while everyone knew where Seed was headed: down, down, down.

Just don't show up, Sautel. You've broken hearts before.

I taste-tested the idea and immediately spit it out. No way I would hurt Kristie. Besides, I wouldn't be breaking her heart—I'd be breaking mine. *I'll just volunteer for my own firing squad at 10:05 p.m. My heart's been headed that way a long time anyway.*

I started my truck, ready to drive home, when all of a sudden it was like my mind . . . slowed . . . way . . . down . . . and then sped up again. *Kristie isn't gonna dump me—she's gonna try to teach me about Jesus!* I realized I didn't have to ditch our date, and if I played my cards right, I might even get to keep seeing her.

Lieutenant Dan's voice from *Forrest Gump* ran through my mind: "Have you found Jesus yet, Gump?"

Followed by Forrest's answer: "I didn't know I was supposed to be looking for him, sir."

I couldn't afford to come across like Forrest. I needed to prepare. If she was going to teach me, I needed to be a good student. But I'd dropped out of high school my sophomore year—or as I called it, my senior year.

Okay, dummy, where can you learn about Jesus without talking to a Christian?

I peeled out of the parking lot. Ten minutes later I braked to a stop outside the Barnes & Noble bookstore where I was supposed to meet Kristie later that night. I'd been inside a few times to grab coffee or people-watch to take my mind off things. But now, as I looked around, I was staggered by the number of books inside. Did people actually *read* all of those?

My mission was clear. I had to search for a book about Jesus. Normally, when I did a search, it was in a smoke-filled room with zero visibility and high heat. This place wasn't much better. But if I started crawling up and down the aisles, blindly swinging my arms and yelling, "Is anyone there?" someone would call the cops.

Seeing as this was my first bookstore rodeo, I fell back on my fire-department training. Instead of finding the saltiest-looking old-school fireman, I found the bookstore equivalent: a sweet old lady behind the counter. Her flowered dress, her glasses perched on the tip of her nose, and her intense stare as she opened the cover of a book told me this ol' gal had plenty of bookstore salt. Perfect.

"Excuse me, can you tell me where I can find a book about Jesus?" I asked.

She laughed. "You need a new Bible, son?"

"Yes, ma'am," I said quickly. "I wore my last one out from all the thumbing I did with it."

She laughed again. "Well, that's just marvelous. Try over there."

I looked where she was pointing and thanked her. *Christian Living? Now* there's *an oxymoron!*

Arriving at the shelves, I quickly scanned the titles. Seemed like "Christian Living" meant a whole bunch of things, including dieting, getting rich, and praying on the toilet every morning. The only thing missing was a book called *Seven Foolproof Ways to Impress a Hot Christian Girl with Your Knowledge of Jesus.*

When the little old lady snuck up and tapped my shoulder, I jumped about a foot. I stared at her. She just pointed again to a different shelf, then bustled back behind the counter. I followed her direction and found the shelves labeled "Bibles." *Go big or go home, Sautel.* I reached out and grabbed the biggest honking one I could find. It had a black leather cover stamped with a golden cross and the letters "KJV," whatever that meant.

Of course the little old lady was the only available cashier. "So," she said, as she rang me up, "tell me about the day you were baptized."

"Ma'am, I'm not a Baptist," I answered, hoping that made some kind of sense.

She laughed again. "You know, our church could use some young blood like you. What church do you go to now?"

"I go to the one up the street with the big cross on it."

Another laugh.

She really needed to get out more if she thought I was that funny. "Keep the change," I said, handing her a few bills, "and thanks for helping me."

Then I grabbed my new Bible and cut! If I could make it out of the store and back to my truck without seeing anyone I knew, my secret would be safe—assuming I made it home un-smited.

—◇—

I yanked open the curtains in my living room and flopped down on the couch. *You got this, Sautel. Finding out about Jesus will be worth it. Focus on Kristie and get after it.*

Page one: "The Holy Bible."

Page two: blank.

Page three: "The Holy Bible containing the Old and New Testaments translated out of the original tongues and with the former translations diligently compared and revised. Authorized King James Version. Red-Letter Edition."

Page four: a bunch of tiny words about who'd published the Bible.

Pages five and six: some sort of letter from some translators to King James.

Page seven: "Table of Contents."

What the . . . Was there actually a Bible *in this Bible?*

Pages eight, nine, ten, and—finally—eleven: "Genesis Chapter One."

Even I knew Genesis was at the beginning of the Bible. I started to read, and twenty minutes later all I'd learned was that Adam and Eve screwed up a pretty sweet arrangement and that whoever wrote the Bible made it sound a lot like some crazy Shakespeare play.

Thirty minutes after that I closed my Bible and tossed it onto the coffee table with a *smack*. What was the point? Sure, I was highly motivated to learn about Jesus before meeting up with Kristie that night, but there was no point pretending to know something I didn't. I was on page thirty-six out of what seemed like a million, and I still didn't have a clue about who Jesus was or if I believed in him.

So instead of reading further, I thought about Kristie. About the kind of love she'd shown me in the few short weeks since we met. When I was nervous, she took the time to make me comfortable. When I messed up, she accepted my messiness. When I didn't know what to say, she would take the awkwardness out of the awkward silence with a hug, a smile, or a joke. Her actions made the word *love* into something more than a word. I'd always wanted to be loved like that, but I'd given up on ever getting it. Ever deserving it. Until Kristie. I could *feel* her love, and it was as real and solid as anything I'd ever known.

I smiled.

Then I thought about the way her tanned legs looked when she wore a skirt. That made me smile even more. *Slow your roll, Sautel.*

I got back to thinking about who she was. It was like the love inside her was better—or bigger, like it was supersized love. Every time I talked to her it felt like she was tapped into some cosmic keg of love, and she could just keep filling my glass over and over and over. She was relentless in how she could look at people and situations with hope instead of despair.

I just didn't know what all that had to do with Jesus—or with me. But then I had a brain wave. *Relax, Sautel. It's all good.* Either I was right, and Kristie was going to teach me about Jesus, or I was wrong, and Kristie was going to dump me. No sense in worrying about it ahead of time. A sense of peace showed up and stuck around.

I couldn't lie or even learn my way through this one. I'd just have to live it.

—◇—

It was 9:55 p.m. Ten minutes early was better than one minute late.

The bookstore was almost empty, apart from the café. Thankfully, the little old lady's shift had ended, so I wouldn't need to give her a Bible update. Clearly I'd picked the wrong book to learn about Jesus, because whoever King James was, his version wasn't great.

At the café I ordered Kristie her white chocolate mocha, plus a water for myself, and then I settled at a table. Kristie arrived exactly when she'd said she would. And since I was trained to size up and evaluate people quickly and accurately, my heart dropped onto the café floor when I saw her. I looked down at my heart with pity. If it was still beating in the next few minutes, I'd stomp on it and put it out of its misery.

As Kristie walked toward me, her shining eyes were full of tears and her hands were shaking. Her hands were shaking like I had seen other people's hands shake a hundred times before, just as I was getting ready to tell them what they already knew: "Your loved one is dead."

This was obviously going to be the last time I would see her. I'd known this day would eventually arrive, but I'd allowed myself to hope it wouldn't be so soon. My mistake. Obviously my honesty that morning had ruined my chances. I leaned forward on the table as she arrived, gesturing at the drink I'd ordered for her. She sat down.

I wanted to say something. Maybe I could plead my case or beg for forgiveness or tell her about the ginormous Bible I'd purchased. But I was hurting too much to speak. The pain made me realize I was in love with her—and then the pain got worse when I realized

I'd never be able to tell her that. There was no way I'd be able to get any words out.

"Jason," she finally asked, "will you please look at me for just a second?"

I dragged my eyes up to meet her wet ones.

She reached both hands out toward me. I started to pull my arms back, but she grabbed my hands first and squeezed.

"Jason," she said. "Jason, I've fallen in love with you." She pulled back a hand to wipe both her cheeks, a thumb across her left, then across her right. "But—"

I froze.

Her free hand took mine again. "But Jason?" she continued. "I won't date you unless you come to church with me."

It was like I was looking at a mirror. Except this time she was the one who couldn't take her eyes off the tabletop and the one feeling the pain of a breaking heart. That stuff was what *I* was supposed to be doing—so I did what Kristie was supposed to do.

"Hey," I said, "look at me for a second."

A small part of my mind acknowledged the oddness. I rarely asked someone to look at me. And when I did, usually it was because that person was about to die a painful death and I wanted to give them a scrap of peace.

She dragged her eyes up, and all I could find in them was sadness and disappointment.

"You," I clarified, "are in love? With *me*?"

She nodded yes. More tears.

"And you want *me* to go to church with you?"

Another nod yes.

That was the exact moment part of my mind noted the time of death: 10:13 p.m. in a bookstore café in Santa Rosa. My black hole had just died. Flatlined. And I knew—somehow I *knew*—it could never be resuscitated.

"Kristie," I said, "I'm in love with you too."

More tears and a hopeful smile. That was a good enough sign that I plowed ahead. "And listen, if going to church is all it takes for me to stay with a hot chick like you, I'm in!"

The laugh that burst out of her was all sorts of sobby, but it *was* a laugh still. And I followed with one of my own.

Then I kept right on talking. "And about the Jesus thing? I bought a Bible today, here, from a little old lady in a flowered dress. I told her I went to church and that I wore my old Bible out. I bought the biggest one I could find, and then I took it home and tried to read it. But it didn't make any sense, and I didn't find anything about Jesus in it, and that's why I'm sitting here with you right now."

She laughed a real laugh. Then she stared disbelievingly at me and asked, "You lied to some sweet old lady and bought a Bible and tried to read it because you thought you were going to lose me?"

I grinned like a puppy.

"I mean, I should say something Christiany here," she said, "but honestly? That is *so* hot!"

I laughed, but then I got serious. "Don't take this wrong," I said, "but it's whatever I see shining out of you that made me do it. When I first saw you in the restaurant, I could see there was something different in you. Whatever that was has only gotten brighter when I'm with you. I can't lose that goodness and love. It's like nothing I've ever felt. There's a . . . a *completeness* about you that gives me something I've never had. You're giving me hope, Kristie."

She looked at me like I was going to keep talking, but that speech was about my limit for coherent words about my inner life.

So I made what I hoped was a smooth transition into joking that was actually flirting. "I guess what I'm saying is that," I continued, "your total hotness is just a huge bonus. So even if I'm being blinded by love and you're actually ugly, I'm cool with that."

"Hey!" she scolded. But it was the good kind of scold. The flirty kind. *Yes! Time to plow ahead with some more serious stuff.* What was happening to me?

"Before I met you," I told her, "everything good in my life always disappeared. I never had a chance to keep it around. The emptiness inside me would either destroy it or chase it off. At my darkest, I went to church, but they told me to leave. And wait until I tell you about the time I cursed out a pastor in my firehouse who showed up to check on my well-being."

Kristie looked into me. Her elbow rested on the table, her chin on her hand.

"Why are you looking at me like that?" I asked.

"Do you remember our first date at Giuseppe's Grotto? When I rambled and you just stared at me?"

"Yeah?"

"You told me how much you enjoyed it and didn't want me to stop. That's what I'm feeling right now. I just want to keep listening, Jason. I want to know everything about you. The good, the bad, the everyday. I love your stories, because I love *you*. I don't love the hurt in them. I don't love you getting hurt. But I guess what I love is how the hurt seems like it's shaping you into something special."

This was uncharted territory for me.

"Jason, people are a mess. You, me, our families, everyone. We're *all* a mess!"

I nodded.

"We all mess up, right? We all fail. I fail. But that guy you were looking for earlier today? Jason, Jesus is the only one who doesn't fail. He can't. He won't. I promise you."

What she was saying made absolutely no sense. To me, Jesus wasn't even real. How could a person have never failed, never messed up? And yet what she was saying *felt* absolutely right. It felt like it made perfect sense. Because from where I was sitting, what other way could I explain what was happening to me?

"Being a Christian doesn't make everything here better," Kristie said. "It doesn't erase pain. But the hope I have through my faith in Jesus? That gives me the strength to keep pushing. And the love Jesus gives me? It can overcome anything. *Everything.*"

I could sniff out a lie in a hot second. Like the time I asked over the phone if she liked sushi and she said yes. And I'd instantly asked her not to lie to me, even if she was just being polite. Whatever Kristie was saying now, she wasn't lying. She might have been spinning me a fairy tale, but if so, the fairy tale was somehow true.

"Anyway," she continued, "I've got like three hours of homework. Then I have school at seven in the morning, and I'm working the lunch and dinner shifts tomorrow. So I've got to run." She started to stand.

"Wait!" I pleaded. "Stay a little longer."

"Don't get all pouty on me, Jason. It'll be Sunday soon, and you and I have a date."

"Hang on, this place is crawling with brainiacs like you, so check this out. Here's how a tenth-grade dropout with a PhD from the University of the Streets of Oakland gets stuff done."

I made eye contact and nodded upward to grab the attention of the guy beside us. He had his face buried in a pile of books but lifted off his headphones to look at me.

"Bro, you wanna make a quick two hundred bucks by knocking out a little nursing homework for this lovely young lady?"

Kristie stood all the way up. "Stop it!" she snapped at me, before turning to the man and apologizing. Then she grabbed my hand and dragged me out of the bookstore. When we hit the sidewalk, she started to give me the business. "You are an idiot, Jason Sautel. You know that? A cute and adorable idiot!"

The look she gave me was the purest thing I had ever seen.

I cupped my hands on her face and wiped away the wetness on her cheeks.

When I pulled her forward and kissed her long and slow and she kissed me back, I knew in my bones that this broken fireman was being put back together. And I knew that whatever was doing the fixing—love, maybe, or even this Jesus guy Kristie believed in—wasn't going to leave me until I was whole again.

CHAPTER 18

THE FIREHOUSE AND THE WORLD OUTSIDE

"SIR, SLOW DOWN AND tell me where the fire is."

"Thirteenth and Broadway!"

The dispatcher's voice woke me from a deep sleep. The new kid we were training bolted out of his bed and took off toward the apparatus bay.

"Slow down, kiddo," I said. "We aren't due yet."

Unless it turned into a second alarm, that is, which required backup. Downtown, where this fire was located, normally didn't get a ton of serious fires. But when they did, they usually needed a ton of backup. High-rise fires are never jokes.

Pretty soon we learned the rookie was right—and with Jimmy enjoying a day off, this kid was going to get some real action.

Less than ten minutes later, me, Cappy, Rog, and the rookie pulled up on scene. Four engines and three ladder trucks had responded to what turned out to be a twenty-story office building. Large-diameter supply hoses connected the engines to hydrants, and smaller-diameter hand lines stretched from each engine into the building, making the street look like someone had spilled a large bowl of pasta on it. Black smoke billowed out of the first-floor windows and doors as well as from the metal grates in the sidewalk. A downtown basement fire was *not* good—and maybe it had already spread to the first floor.

Cappy went to chat it up with the battalion chief. Me and the rookie pulled a hose line toward the ground floor door while Rog got us hooked up to water. The rookie grabbed the 2.5-inch hose line—a beast to carry, but big fires called for bigger hoses and *lots* of water—as I jogged to the door. It had already been popped by another crew. I stuck my head in but couldn't see any fire. The other crews were already in the basement fighting the fire, so I needed to check this floor. Unless the nozzle crews below us knocked down the fire, it would soon be spreading up, up, and up.

"Kid, wait here," I ordered. "I'm gonna do a quick recon. Do *not* go inside!"

Before we committed our line, I wanted a better sense of where we might want to deploy on the first floor. Normally it took four guys to properly advance the heavier 2.5-inch hose line, but since Rog and Cappy were busy elsewhere, we didn't have that luxury. Wherever me and the rookie went, we had to get it right the first time.

I tugged on my mask and advanced alone, hopping to see a telltale glow. Smoke was pushing down, and visibility was rapidly deteriorating. I got lower and kept pushing. I felt some water pooling on the ground as I crawled through but still didn't see any flames. But that didn't mean there was no fire on the first floor, just that I hadn't found it yet. I kept pushing straight ahead, then hit a wall. I stopped. There were twenty-some floors above me, a burning basement below me, and I was alone with no hose line and no sense of where the fire was or might be coming from.

Turn back. All my senses weirded out at once. *Turn back.*

I started to crawl back the way I'd come when flames descended through the darkness. What had been only smoke was now an inferno. Floor to ceiling, like a curtain of fire had been pulled down.

I had no radio. No hose line. No exit. And trying to crawl through the wall of flames would kill me in four or five seconds. I had only one option. Curling in a fetal position on my side, my face toward a wall and my back toward the curtain of fire, I slowed my breathing, forcing myself to calm down and conserve oxygen. It would be a minute or two before I burned to death, which was much better than four or five seconds!

Nice going, Sautel. You finally got to a place where you're happy, and now you're gonna die. In all your years of dumb decisions, this is riiight up there.

A short while back I would have been ready for death. But now that I was dying, I felt like I had a life to live. Did that count as ironic? Seemed like I'd finally been given a chance at everything I'd been longing for but had given up hoping for. Love. Acceptance. A future that was maybe lighter than it was dark. I'd been craving all that ever since I was just a ten-year-old kid considering suicide—and every single day since.

I want to not die. I want to see Kristie. I want to see what happens next.

Everything was hot. Everything hurt. My legs began to blister. I looked down and discovered flames covering my boots and clinging to the legs of my turnout pants. *Huh.* That should have been impossible. Turnout pants didn't catch fire until *after* the firefighter was already dead.

Wait, am I dead?

If not, I would be soon. I sucked in my first deep breath in a couple minutes, briefly lifted my face mask, and screamed, "Mayday! Mayday! Mayday!" In firefighting terms that meant, "Attention, anyone who can hear. I don't mean to be a bother, but I'm about to die."

Face mask back on. Eyes closed. One deep breath, and then slower, slower, slower breaths. I still had a bit of air, so technically I still had hope. My turnout coat was starting to burn, along with my pants and boots. I curled as tight as I could.

Then a distant part of my mind registered the beautiful, battering sound of a hose line going toe to toe with old man fire. Next came the sound of someone shouting my name and the *shlurp*-shuffle of a pack of fire boots arriving.

Still fetal, I opened my eyes to a circle of white light on the scorched floor. A firefighter's knee touched down in the circle of light. I squinted up at a silhouette. Then I was getting hauled to my feet by a set of strong hands.

"Sautel," growled Cappy's unmistakable voice, "you are dumb. As. A. Brick."

"Cappy," I said. "*Cappy.*"

"Kid's delirious," he chuckled. "Probably from soaking up an entire floor of flammable photo chemicals. No wonder he was lit up like a firework!"

—◇—

We got back to the station around five in the morning. I went to the kitchen, dropped a pot of coffee, cleaned my gear, and then hit the showers.

I was shook up good.

I'd been in a lot of tight spots. I'd seen plenty of people die—and had been on the verge of death myself—but I'd never been scared like I was that morning. Maybe it was because I'd always had a way to bail. Like with the woman who'd fallen from her hospital bed. I *could* have jumped back out the window and left her inside. I hadn't, but I could have. Or maybe it was because I'd never felt like my life was valuable enough to save.

What now? What had changed that had me so freaked out? I pictured the curtain of flame coming closer and closer. I tasted the fear of having no way out, of being helpless in a trap.

Kristie and I had been dating for about a month. What Kristie was teaching me, and what I was hearing at the little church we started going to together, was beginning to make sense. In some ways it was just different words for what I already knew from experience. The messed-up, broken-down world I knew so well was fallen. Sinful. And the times of peace, the genuine love, was God. I got it.

The world around me was still full of sadness, but it just didn't seem so *dark* anymore. My past was full of pain. That would never change. But it didn't feel like it defined me anymore, or like it ever could again. I didn't hear a heavenly choir. Honestly, I didn't even feel anything different. All I knew was that nearly dying in that high-rise was a turning point. So I prayed.

God, it's me. Sautel. I almost died today, which I guess you already know. But if I'd died before putting my faith in Jesus and what He did for me . . . I can't imagine. I can't let that happen. God, thanks for chasing me all these years.

That was it.

I noted the time of life: 6:37 a.m. in OFD Station 11 on the west side of Oakland.

─◇─

When I told Kristie, it was no big deal. Like she'd already guessed. Maybe she had.

Kristie hadn't saved me. It wasn't like that. I knew God had done all the saving. She had just shown me it was possible. That being saved could happen to anyone, even a guy as screwed up as me. I was still a guy who rescued people, shift after shift after shift. That hadn't changed. But the rescuer had been rescued.

Kristie was rummaging through the empty cupboards in the kitchen of my place in Santa Rosa, looking for a coffee cup.

I cleared my throat and held up the cup I was using. "Already in use," I told her.

She stuck her hands on her hips and gave me a serious look. *She is so stinking beautiful.* "Jason, you're telling me you have *one* coffee cup?"

"Yep," I answered. I opened a drawer. "One spoon, one fork, one knife. Getting the idea? And look in this cupboard here. One plate and one bowl!"

She looked like she either wanted to kiss me or kill me. Probably kill me.

"Okay, okay," I said nicely. "I got a full set in a box somewhere. I just never needed them."

"Well, now you do," she said. "Now *we* do."

It took me longer to tell Rog, Jimmy, and Cappy.

One night we got back to the firehouse and sat down for a meal of cold steaks and wilted Caesar salad. Three hours before it had been fresh, but no sooner had we sat down that dispatch called us to a fire. Now, with our cold dinner in front of us, I was jamming up Jimmy, who had pulled two hundred feet of hose line even though Rog had parked the engine only twenty feet from the fire.

"Bro, I spent more time knocking the kinks out of that hose pull of yours than I spent in the house fighting fire with you!"

Cappy and Rog were laughing. This was the kind of banter we lived for.

"Better to have too much than come up short!" retorted Jimmy. "Kinda the story of your life, right?"

"Funny, but a plate of spaghetti in someone's front yard never helped put out a fire!"

"Seed, plenty of times on scene you're even *less* helpful than a plate of spaghetti."

Cappy and Rog were still laughing. I zipped my lips.

"C'mon, Seed," Jimmy egged me on. "Ball's in your court. Fire back!"

I just smiled and chowed down on my bowl of withered salad and soggy croutons.

"Cappy," asked Jimmy, "what's wrong with our Demon Seed? I know silence can be a great comeback, but he *never* uses that tactic!"

I took a few more bites, then finally hopped back in. "Bro, you're right. Silence can be a very effective tactic, especially against you when you *know* you screwed up on a fire. Losers hate the silent treatment. I get it."

Cappy raised his eyebrows. He was loving it.

"And bro," I continued, "me sitting here quiet gives you time to reflect on how lame your hose move was. But as much as that brings a smile to my face, that's not why I'm doing it."

Cappy nudged Rog. He lived and breathed tactics and could tell I was about to open up the bomb bay doors and drop something big right on Jimmy's plate. But not even Cappy knew what was coming.

"You ever seen a mustard seed?" I asked, holding the tip of my right thumb right next to the tip of my forefinger. "I was the Demon Seed, but something as small as a mustard seed can change even the most hard-core of men. The guy you're looking at isn't the same one you've been working with all these years. I've been equipped with a whole new set of ammunition to drop on you, so check this—I'm not sitting here quietly because I want you to reflect on your stupid move of pulling ten times the hose we needed."

The three guys were just gaping at me. *Nuke time.*

"Jimmy, I'm sitting here quietly because I was remembering a Bible verse I heard in church last week with Kristie. 'Fools vent their anger, but the wise quietly hold it back.'"

For the first time in my memory, Cappy lost his cool. He coughed an actual piece of steak from his mouth. It landed on the table with a small, wet sound. After a long second, he cleared his throat and said, "Well, damn, but if I ever needed proof that miracles can happen . . ." He shrugged, then finished his thought, "Now I got my proof."

Jimmy just shook his head and gave a small smile. It was a lot for him to process, but he'd come around.

And Rog? He was grinning fit to split his cheeks, like he'd just seen a nonbreathing victim unexpectedly start sucking down air. He didn't say a word—just stuck his fist across the table and bumped mine. He probably could've cited the chapter and verse for what I'd just thrown at Jimmy—Proverbs 29:11—but dispatch let us know that the world outside the firehouse needed us again.

"Ma'am, what's burning and where are you?"

We all listened.

"The house next door, in the four thousand block of Market street!"

We would. We did. I wolfed one more bite of stale salad and washed it down with room-temperature soda. Less than a minute later, the four of us were rolling down the street on the engine. I spun and stood to catch a view and saw the column of smoke a few blocks away. Jimmy was standing too. We shared a look.

"I love this job!" I yelled.

"We got a worker, boys!" Cappy hollered from the front seat.

Beside me Jimmy howled like a maniac as Rog gunned the engine around a tight corner.

Just another hot night in Oakland.

ACKNOWLEDGMENTS

I CAN'T BELIEVE YOU'RE reading these acknowledgments because that means you finished my book. And that I actually wrote a book! This means I have a ton of people to thank.

I want to thank you, Mom and Dad. As a parent myself, I'm learning over and over how stinking hard it is to raise kids. I can't imagine doing it alone without a solid community. When I was a kid I didn't know what to do with all my stressors, so I just shut down. And later, I took it out on you. I'm sorry for my part in our pain. I love both of you, and I appreciate the grace you have shown as God continues to work on me.

I want to thank the men and women of the Oakland Fire Department. The day the doc told me I couldn't be a firefighter anymore because of my injury, the shame I felt from having to leave a career and the people I loved so much made me panic. Honestly that was the single worst day of my life. If I walked away without saying goodbye, that's on me, not you. And I want those of you I was so blessed to work alongside to know this: there isn't a single day that goes by that I don't think about our laughs, our fights, and the honest conversations we shared around the firehouse dinner table. You worked harder than me, longer than me, and performed way more courageous acts than the few I wrote about in this book. When my kids ask me what heroes look like, I point them to you, the diverse and badass group of men and women who are the Oakland Fire Department.

You wouldn't be holding this book unless Tawny Johnson, my rock-star agent, had believed in me and my story. Tawny, you took a chance on a guy who wasn't an author. And honestly, if I were you I would've hung up the phone after our first conversation and changed my number! You mean the world to my family and me. I'll never not be grateful. You and the team at Illuminate Literary are the best. (Hi, Marty and Jenni!)

You also wouldn't be holding this book without my writer, David Jacobsen. David, I know you like the D. R. thing, bro, but you ain't a doctor! You showed me a ton of patience, a ton of grace, and most of all, you helped me sound like me, not like some fancy author with an overpaid education. Your ability to keep me (relatively) focused is a rare skill set. I'm still in awe of the way you took my conversion story out of my brain and heart and brought it to life for others to read.

Thank you to my team at Nelson Books: Jessica Wong, Sujin Hong, Phoebe Wetherbee, Chernal Patton, Rachel Tockstein, Shea Nolen, Claire Drake, Jamie Lockard, and Timothy Paulson, and the many people behind the scenes, including my proofreader, Whitney Bak—props to her for writing my very first 5-star review! It was an honor to work with and learn from all of you. I still wake up and ask Kristie if this is really happening. Seriously, *me*? When you guys signed me, I started to panic because I suddenly remembered that the last English class I took was in the tenth grade. My deepest apologies go out to the editing department. Unfortunately I still have no idea what an adverb is, but I am pretty solid when it comes to Proverbs at least!

To my kids, Beth, Alex, Isaac, and Noah. This story is as much yours as it is mine. You are four of the biggest reasons God faithfully kept calling me toward Jesus. God knew that you guys needed me and that I needed you! Each of you motivates me in a different way, blesses me in a different way. I will never stop loving you as hard as I can.

And Kristie. Kristie, without you I wouldn't be typing out these acknowledgments. Every time I wanted to throw in the towel and hit the delete button because I didn't feel capable or good enough, you would lovingly tell me to take a break—and then pray for me until I was ready to roll again. I can't thank God enough for you. You are who I learn from, who I grow with, who smacks me when I need it, and who is more beautiful and more amazing every single day of our lives together. Kristie, I love you.

To Daisy Mae and Gronk, thank you! You are a very good girl and a very good boy. Yes, you are! And Bosco. Unfortunately, after eighteen years of being my best friend, you passed away as I was writing this book. You were always there to greet me as I came through the door from a rough shift, you were at my side when I proposed to Kristie, and you watched over our family during my long shifts at the firehouse. Thank you for the memories, buddy. I can't wait to play fetch with you again one day.

And lastly, and most importantly, God, I thank you. I am not sure how to properly acknowledge the love You have graced me with using words alone, so when I am done typing, I will be with You in prayer. As I was writing the conversion story You gave me, I constantly reflected on the fear of what my eternity would have looked like if I died a faithless man. That fear, along with the absolute awe and pure love I have for You, helped me stay the course, even on the days I wanted to give up. My hope is that my story will glorify You and bring others to the same hope and saving faith I found in Jesus.

ABOUT THE AUTHOR

JASON SAUTEL spent twenty-two years working as a paramedic and firefighter, but his fondest memories are from his time serving the citizens of Oakland as a member of the Oakland Fire Department. Today he shares Christ-centered stories and lessons through his writing, speaking, and social media platform. He loves his wife of sixteen years, Kristie, his four two-legged children, and his two four-legged children. He also appreciates God's good gifts of donuts, surfing, and Maui. You can reach him at gracefullyrescued@gmail.com.

ABOUT THE WRITER

D. R. JACOBSEN is a collaborative writer who helps entrepreneurs, pastors, parents, business leaders, athletes, professors, first responders, and other ordinary people with extraordinary stories to tell. He holds a BA in English from Westmont College, an MA in theology from Regent College, and an MFA in creative writing from Seattle Pacific University. He is the author of *Rookie Dad* and is represented by Tawny Johnson of Illuminate Literary Agency (illuminateliterary.com). Jacobsen and his wife have lived in California, Austria, and British Columbia, and they now make their home, with their two boys, in central Oregon. You can connect with him at jacobsenwriting.com